ANTHROPOLOGICAL PAPERS

MUSEUM OF ANTHROPOLOGY, UNIVERSITY OF MICHIGAN

NO. 44

PROPERTY CONTROL AND SOCIAL STRATEGIES: SETTLERS ON A MIDDLE EASTERN PLAIN

BY

BARBARA C. ASWAD

ANN ARBOR

THE UNIVERSITY OF MICHIGAN, 1971

PROPERTY CONTROL AND SOCIAL STRATEGIES IN
SETTLERS IN A MIDDLE EASTERN PLAIN

PREFACE

THE material presented here is based on field work in villages in southern Turkey along the Syrian border, where I lived for ten months from the beginning of September, 1964, to the end of June, 1965. The trip was made possible through a Fulbright Graduate Research Grant.

I owe extreme gratitude to the many villagers of the area of study, and in particular to the Al Shiukh tribal group in whose villages I resided, and to Ayush, the marvelous woman and friend who shared her home and life with me in the village. Also, I want to thank the many friends and relatives in Antakya who made my visits to that city pleasant and Salim who helped me in translating. A word of thanks is due to Dr. Halil Inalcik of Ankara University for aiding me with Ottoman documents in Turkey, and to the many officials in various departments of the government of Turkey who assisted me.

I especially want to thank various professors and colleagues for their assistance and encouragement during the periods of preparation of this research. In particular I wish to thank my professors at the University of Michigan, William D. Schorger of the Center for Near Eastern and North African Studies and the Department of Anthropology and Eric Wolf of the Department of Anthropology, for their instruction, assistance and patience. I also want to thank Louise Sweet, Marvyn Meggitt and Marshall Sahlins for their inspiration, encouragement and comments on the manuscript, and Arnold Pilling for his constructive criticisms. I am indebted to James Stewart-Robinson and to my father-in-law, Abdulkader Aswad, for their aid in the translation of Ottoman documents. And last but not least, I should like to extend my gratitude to Marie Wilt for typing and proofreading and to Joanne Bailis and Lynne Sweeney for the editing. My thanks also go to Joan Enerson, who drew Map 1 and many of the figures.

To my parents and my husband Adnan, whose sacrifice, patience and encouragement have been invaluable to me, I dedicate this work.

The study was originally prepared and submitted in partial fulfillment of the requirements for the degree of doctor of philosophy to the Department of Anthropology of the University of

Michigan in 1968. Parts of the original have been rewritten. However, the basic analysis remains the same. I am appreciative of the financial support which permits this monograph to be published. It was furnished by the Center for Near Eastern and North African Studies of the University of Michigan jointly with the Museum of Anthropology.

In translating Arabic words to English, I follow the system adopted by the Encyclopedia of Islam, with the following exceptions: ḳ is written q, dj is written j and proper names are not marked with long vowels. In the use of Turkish words, soft g and undotted i have been replaced by their English approximations.

The majority of the material discussed here is from one village, supplemented by data from three neighboring villages. To avoid complications, fictitious names have been given to the tribal sections which are analyzed in detail, i.e., the Al Shiukh and those societies, villages and persons described in Chapters Three and Four.

Measurements are given in terms of the units used in the area. Donums (for land measurement) can be converted to acres at the rate of 4 donums to 1 acre. There are 2.2 pounds in a kilo, 1.6 kilometers in a mile, and in 1964-65 the official rate of exchange of the Turkish Lira (TL) was 9.4 TL to $1.00 U.S.

Village maps (Figs. 3 and 4) were made in 1925-27 by the French Mandate Government, Travaux du Cadastre et d'Amelioration Agricole des Etats de Syrie, du Liban, et des Alouites and are 1/2,000 and 1/5,000 respectively. Figure 2 is also from the Travaux. The maps and photo were made available through the courtesy of the University of Chicago and through the Tapu Defterli Office in Turkey.

TABLE OF CONTENTS

Introduction 1

I. Historical and Ecological Setting 3
    Ecology and the Distribution of Peoples in the
        Hatay Province 9
    The Amik Plain 16

II. The Struggle for Land and the Organization of
    Villages in the Plain 21
    Turkman Settlement into the Estate System 29
    Al Shiukh Settlement into Core and Fringe Villages 38

III. Patterns of Descent, Inheritance and Marriage
    Among the Al Shiukh 47
    Descent and Inheritance Rules 47
    Bridewealth (Naqd) 57
    Vengeance 61
    Marriage Patterns According to Rank and Landholdings . . 62
    Polygyny and the Dispersal Ratio of Marriages 66

IV. Marriage and Other Alliances by the Al Shiukh in the
    Struggle for the Control of Resources:
    A Diachronic Analysis 75
    Variance in Marriage Patterns Over Five Generations . . . 75
    Principles of Descent Group Discord Continuity:
        Marriages and other Strategies 78
    A Diachronic Examination of the Cases 85
    Behavioral Patterns in Light of Alliance Formations . . . 104

V. Conclusion 111

Appendixes 117
    A. Nineteenth Century Ottoman Tapu Defter Describing
        the Settlement of the Reyhanli Confederation 117
    B. Ottoman Land Classifications 121
    C. Types of Work Contracts in the Hatay 123
    D. Settlement Pattern of Sharecroppers' Mud and Reed
        Houses on a Turkman Estate: A Freehand Sketch . . . 125
    E. Annual Agricultural Work Cycle 127
    F. Income Distribution of Three Villages 129
    G. Annual Village Income for Core Village 131
    H. Annual Village Expenditures for Core Village 133
    I. Tests to Isolate Size Factor in Marriage Preference
        Patterns within the Al Shiukh Patronymic Section . . . 135

CONTENTS

J. Observed Minus Expected Frequency Choices by Sublineage among the Al Shiukh, Two and one half Generations 137
K. Index of Preference of Sublineage I for Marriage with Sublineage J among the Al Shiukh, Two and one half Generations. 139
L. Observed Minus Expected Frequency Distribution of Marriage Choices by Lineage among the Al Shiukh, Four and one half Generations 141
M. Index of Preference of Lineage I for Marriage with Lineage J among the Al Shiukh, Four and one half Generations 141

Bibliography. 143

LIST OF TABLES

1. Marriage Patterns of a Turkman Landlord Lineage 32
2. Marriages of Sharecropping and Working Men on a Turkish Estate 35
3. Marriages of Arabic-Speaking Tribal Sections Living in the Same Region but Differing in Status, Amoung of Land Owned and Localization of Kin 63
4. Patterns of Village Endogamy and Exogamy 64
5. Marriage Dispersal Ratio by Tribal Sections 67
6. Marriage Dispersal Ratio by Lineages of the Al Shiukh 67
7. Marriage Dispersal Ratio by Sublineages of the Al Shiukh . . . 68
8. Observed Frequency Distribution of Marriages by Sublineage and Origin of Spouse among the Al Shiukh 69
9. Observed Frequency Distribution of Marriage Choices by Sublineages among the Al Shiukh 70
10. Observed Frequency Distribution of Marriages by Lineage and Origin of Spouse among the Al Shiukh 71
11. Observed Frequency Distribution of Marriage Choices by Lineage among the Al Shiukh 71
12 Total Marriage Patterns Considered by Percentages for Five Generation Levels in Shaykh Salih's Lineage 76
13. Number of Living Descendants of Leaders of Each Generation of the Al Shiukh 85
14. Generation Four Competitors' Children's Marriages by Village 97
15. Land Amounts and Current Size According to Lineage, Sublineage and ᶜAshīret Section 100
16. Land Amounts and Current Size of Groups for Core and Fringe Villages 101

LIST OF FIGURES

1. Ethnic Groups of the Hatay 13

CONTENTS

2. Aerial View of a Nucleated Core Village and its Surrounding Lands 26
3. French Cadastral Map of Stablized Landholdings in a Fringe Village 27
4. French Cadastral Map of a Turkman Estate 28
5. Patronymic Expansion of the Al Shiukh in Core and Fringe Villages: Two Periods 39
6. Model of the Ideal Marriage Patterns Arranged Between Lineage Competitors 80
7. Marriages among Three Al Shiukh Lineages, First and Second Generations 87
8. Movement of Brides in Third Generation Arranged by Chief Lineage Competitors of Second Generation 93
9. Movement of Brides in Fourth Generation Arranged by Chief Lineage Competitors of Third Generation 95

LIST OF PLATES
(Following page 152)

1. Bay of Iskenderun and Amanus Mountain Range.
2. View of a Village.
3. Typical Home of Al Shiukh.
4. House of a Worker or Sharecropper.
5a. Guest Room (Oda), Villagers, Teachers and Coffee Utensils.
5b. Respected Shaykh in Oda.
6. Women at the Well.
7. Storage Bins and Outside Kitchen for Wife of Al Shiukh.
8a. Outside Kitchen for Wife of Shepherd.
8b. Stacked bedding.
9. Seeding in the Traditional Method.
10a. Rented Tractors.
10b. Traditional Scratch Plow and Saluqi Dog.
11a. Cotton Laden on Trucks in the Region.
11b. The Town Market.
12. Measuring Land Divisions with Ropes.
13. Grinding Grain in the Traditional Method.
14. Bee Hives.
15. Village School.
16. Boys going to the City to Trade School and the Lise.
17. Dancing the Debke at a Wedding.

INTRODUCTION

THE object of this study is to carry out a diachronic analysis of the dynamic features of social organization and land control of Middle Eastern tribal societies that have become sedentarized from a perspective of cultural and geographical adaptation. The emphasis is upon the analysis of kinship and marriage and other strategies of mobility involving the control of resources in a period of rapid stratification which involved both sedentarization and increasing commercialization of resources.

Because of the complex nature of a shatter zone such as the region in which the study was conducted, extra attention has been given to the ecological history of the area and groups under study. Chapter One gives a general outline of the cultural history of the Hatay region of Turkey. Chapter Two describes in greater detail the conditions of tribal settlement and land tenure in the Amik Plain during the second half of the nineteenth century and the resulting patterns of land and village organization. Two different systems of stratification developed in the region, the estate pattern and a pattern of competing agnatic core and fringe villages. These systems are compared and analyzed.

Within this wider framework, the remaining chapters provide a detailed analysis of the dynamics of the social organization of a tribal section, the Al Shiukh, who are part of the core and fringe village pattern. Their organization is studied over four and one-half generations, the period since their settlement. This analysis includes changes such as their new position in relation to other rural groups as a result of sedentarization policies and the change to immobile property, their position in relation to the increasing commercialization of resources and their contact with the rising urban landed elites who were acquiring land through purchase and the extension of credit. Finally, the recent effect of cashcropping and the use of mechanized agricultural techniques is discussed. We find that the Al Shiukh have maintained and expanded their control of land in this process by maintaining a position of middlemen or brokers, and their strategies are similar to other groups who have been in this position. For purposes of comparison, data are included on the social organization of other groups in the plain which differ in their socio-economic position from the Al Shiukh.

Since many of the strategies of mobility of this middle group are expressed in kinship and marriage, much attention has been paid to the analysis of marriages in this study. Also, since the marital patterns of one generation indicate the processes of alliance and opposition and the accompanying transfer of money through bridewealth made in the previous generation, only a diachronic analysis can help us understand the processes involved. In this regard, we find that much of the literature on patrilineal parallel cousin marriage and endogamy has been characterized by a lack of detailed data or has been pursued through essentially synchronic analyses. It is hoped that this approach will add to the information on the nature of strategies of mobility and their relation to the processes of marriage, kinship, stratification and social change in the Middle East.

I

HISTORICAL AND ECOLOGICAL SETTING

THE Hatay lies in the northeastern arch of the Fertile Crescent. It is ecologically diverse and its history is characterized by shifting zones of governmental influence, shifting ideological, linguistic and ethnic identifications, and by actual population movements between its constituent zones. Most recently, it shares with the rest of the Middle East the processes of adaptation to the expansion of commercial and industrial systems into the region, in particular that of the western capitalist system.

Through the area have passed the main east-west overland trade routes of the Middle East; and it has constituted a center ground for the repeated historical tugs-of-war between eastern and western empires. The boundary between East and West has often fallen exactly within the region, polarizing it between the city of Antakya (Antioch), oriented towards the West, and the city of Aleppo, oriented towards the East. The Amik Plain, which lies between these two cities, has been the site of recurrent battles. It was into this plain that the main subjects of this study, the Al Shiukh, settled a century ago. The region has no large irrigation-based urban centers and the struggles of larger rival empires have always enmeshed the Hatay. It suffered many times over encroachment and occupation by foreign groups who utilized its larger centers of population as centers of control in trade and taxation; the surpluses of the region often went to support seats of government many miles distant.

As in all the world, various ecological and often primarily geographical factors affect the degree to which local societies are organized by state systems of stratification or by principles of kinship. In the Middle East generally, the areas of direct governmental control, population density and greater social and economic stratification are the cities, the river valleys and some coastal regions. Under past agrarian empires we find that identification with the state by ruling groups within these areas took the form of religious affiliation, which in the case of the Ottoman Empire was Sunni Islam, and to varying degrees the use of

Ottoman Turkish and certain patterns of behavior. On the other hand, societies on the periphery of state control, as well as groups within areas of direct control but which engaged in occupations other than those of land control and administration, and primarily those connected with commerce, often maintained ethnic identities other than those of the ruling strata. This information is important for our understanding of the general distribution of ethnic groups[1] in the Hatay today, so let us continue a bit further into the patterns of the Ottoman Empire, which governed the region for some four hundred years.

We may take as an example the case of the Ottoman politico-economic system of tax farming, which operated in the sixteenth through the mid-nineteenth centuries and which had replaced the more prebendal Ottoman Timar system. During these centuries, we find two different forms of the tax farming system in the region, the *Iltizam* and the *Iqta^c*. Their separate distributions were correlated with ecological factors. The *Iltizam* operated in areas of more direct control and the *Iqta^c* in outlying regions of control, primarily mountainous areas and plains under tribal control. In the *Iltizam* the position of tax collector was bid for and, as Harik described it, "The dignitaries whether war lords, aristocratic chiefs or notables were invested with government authority by an overlord who enjoyed over them the prerogative of appointment and dismissal" (1965:411). Only Sunni Muslims could hold office and become *multizams* (tax farmers). Other occupational categories in these areas, such as those of merchants, translators and bankers in the urban areas, and at times landless sharecroppers in the rural regions, were filled by those of religious identification other than Sunni Muslim. Those involved in trade external to the region or the empire were often Christian or Jewish,[2] while local merchants dealing with desert and mountain regions were usually Muslim. Rural sharecroppers who were not Sunni Muslim were usually not of the Christian or Jewish faith, but rather of other Muslim sects, and would be found in areas adjacent to outlying regions in which they were dominant. For example, they might have migrated from a mountain area to work in a nearby river valley.

In the outlying regions, the control of resources was greatly influenced by kinship alliances and hereditary control. These

---

[1] I am using McKim Mariott's definition of an ethnic group as "a hereditary group within a society which is defined by its members and by others as a separate people, socially, biologically and culturally; it need not be distinguishable in objective fact by any unique complex of cultural or biological traits" (as quoted in Sinha, 1967:92).

[2] Under the Ottomans, Christian and Jewish minorities maintained their own customary laws and judges, who were ultimately responsible to the Sultan's cabinet, and thus maintained some cultural and ethnic autonomy.

areas included groups of varying degrees of rank and status, depending it would seem on the availability of resources and on the density of population, as well as proximity to markets and the urban centers. Along the Mediterranean coast we find societies whose social rank is extensively developed. Their upper classes include both secular and sacred positions of rank which are accompanied by varying amounts of economic privilege. The emphasis upon social rank in these areas may mislead outsiders regarding the extent of economic ranking.[3] These areas include such heterodox Islamic groups as the Druze, the Shi^{c}a of Lebanon, the Nusairis (^{C}Alawis) of Syria and Turkey, and a Christian minority such as the Maronites of Lebanon. It was these areas which were under the Ottoman *Iqṭa^c* system. Harik describes the system for Lebanon: "Authority was distributed among a number of autonomous hereditary aristocratic chiefs subordinate in certain political respects to a common overlord" (1965:405). These elites lived in the rural areas, and while it was the duty of the bureaucrates in the *Iltizam* area to help raise an army for the Sultan, the members of the *Iqṭa^c* had their own personal guards only. Some of the current economic stratification in the areas is recent and is a result of increased market contacts and a limited introduction of machinery. It is also in these areas that we may find what Eric Wolf has termed the "middle peasantry," that is, a peasantry which has "secure access to land of its own and cultivates it with family labor."[4]

Outside of these areas of the *Iltizam* and the *Iqṭa^c*, tribal groups operated for the most part free from taxation, and their rank and status were of a more egalitarian nature than those of the other two systems.

It is interesting to note that historically some groups which were on the periphery of control were considered to have broken from Islam and were often persecuted. They were termed *zindīq*. For example the Yazidi, a ranked sect which lives along the Syrian-Turkish border and who have been called Devil Worshippers, were subject to numerous massacres during the last three centuries of Ottoman rule. Their presence along an important trade route perhaps helps to explain this. For members of these outlying Islamic minority groups, temporary conversion (*taqiya*) allowed their members to take the religious identity of the government whenever they were in areas of strong governmental control.

[3] See Peters (1963) for one discussion of rank and status in Lebanon.
[4] See conclusions, Wolf, 1969:291.

In terms of ecology and religious identification, we may also observe that numerous and varied ranked religious brotherhoods of the Sunni Muslim variety occur along ecological border zones in the rural regions. In our study, the zone that is important to our discussion is that of the Syrian-Turkish border. Some of the names of the societies commonly found in this region are the Qadiriya, Naqshabandi and Rifa^{c}i. The rank of their shaykhs combines both hereditary, temporal and spiritual powers as well as economic privilege. Their shaykhs also know Arabic, the language of Islam, even though members may be native speakers of Kurdish or Turkish. This region historically has been a contact area between urban centers and the countryside since major trade routes cross it. It is also a region where pastures are contested between those who use the mountain regions, usually Kurdish or Turkish speakers, and those of the plains and deserts, usually Arabic speakers. Thus the specialization of the religious shaykhs as mediators is obviously related to their role as brokers between different social and geographical segments.[5]

The main group under discussion in this study, the Al Shiukh, are shaykhs of one of these religious brotherhoods, the Qadiriya,[6] and it would seem that they also share some characteristics with the Yazidi, although any relationship they may have with the latter must for my part remain inferential. Since religious brotherhoods are competitors to urban control in the rural areas, these brotherhoods have been curtailed in recent times due to the extension of urban power. Further information on the historical relationship of the Al Shiukh and the Yazidi in the area is discussed in the footnote below.[7]

---

[5]This function correlates with findings by other authors in other parts of the world: Gellner's study of saints among the Arab-Berber boundaries in Morocco (1963) and Barth's discussion of Pakistan (1965). I prefer to use the term religious shaykh rather than saint due to the numerous differences involved in the social functions and organization of these religious holymen and the saints of Europe to whom the term generally refers.

[6]Qadiriya is an order of dervishes called after Abdul al-Qadir al Jilani (d. 1166), who was the principal of a school of Hanbalite Law in Baghdad. The order is widespread, and is active in such areas as Morocco, Turkey, Iraq and India (Margoliouth, 1965:202-05).

[7]The Yazidi are a ranked border society whose members are considered to be primarily Kurdish. Their religious beliefs are eclectic and combine elements of Zoroastrianism, Christianity and Islam. It is interesting to note in this ranked border community, that the shaykhs, who are the main property owners and mediators, wear the desert Arabic clothes and headdress, speak Arabic and Kurdish and have Arabic names. The Yazidi social segments of lesser rank have Kurdish names, speak only Kurdish, and wear clothes more resembling those of mountain societies than those of desert societies (Lescot, 1938:90, 144). Their main location is along the Turkish-Syrian border from the Hatay to Mosul Iraq, and in eastern Turkey. Jebel Sinjar, in eastern Syria, remains their headquarters, while the majority of those near Aleppo have converted to Sunni Islam. A good account has been written about them by Lescot (1938).

Historically, they were strong in the thirteenth and fourteenth centuries. The Emirs of the Jazira were Yazidi, as was one of the Emirs of Damascus (Lescot, 1938:105). They were also dominant in the Afrine Valley which leads to the Amik Plain, in the rule of the Kurdish Ayyubid ruler, Salah al-Din, in the twelfth century. Later the Ottoman government schools recruited many Yazidi who converted to Sunni Islam while the mountain Yazidi maintained their faith (Lescot, 1938:108). Minorsky (1913:1145) reports: "The ruling dynasty (at Killis) believed it was related to those of Hakkari and ^{c}Amadiya. Their ancestor Mand (Mantasha) had rendered services to the Aiybids who gave him the control of Kusair and those living between Hama and Mar^{c}ash as well as the Kurds of Djom and Killis. Under the Mamluk Sultans and under Selim I disputes broke out between the Yazidis

HISTORICAL AND ECOLOGICAL SETTING

We have indicated some of the historical, socio-economic and political patterns. In the mid-nineteenth and the twentieth centuries, the increased commercialism and the presence of western political control in the form of a mandate power in the twentieth century gave rise to new segments of power, one of which was a commercialized landed elite. Most of the large families that rose during this period were members of locally powerful families or of the bureaucracy. They obtained land titles and in the rural areas, kin groups united and joined in the struggle for the acquisition of titles. There were conversions to Sunni Islam by those who found it necessary or convenient in obtaining these land titles.

Minorities were placed in the bureaucracy by the mandate powers, and the increased trade with Europe also strengthened the political and economic position of certain minorities. In the mid-twentieth century, Christian tractor merchants began to buy lands in Syria as the spread of modern agricultural practices and cashcropping of cotton became lucrative. In Syria this latter pattern has been reduced recently due to the land reforms and socialistic policies of the government. The Hatay has special historical characteristics which separate it from the particular history of either Turkey or Syria, for the region was a portion of Syria in the early twentieth century under French mandate when some Turkish reforms were occurring; and in 1939 it became part of Turkey, and thus did not enter into the socialistic reforms of Syria. The change in political status of the region in 1939 was accompanied by emigration by certain groups, particularly Christian groups. Thus the role which was filled by Christian merchants in Syria was held by other groups in the Hatay, some being local landlords and others being merchants from central Turkey. We shall elaborate on these ethnic migrations in more detail later, however we may comment here that although there is no perfect correlation between ethnic location

---

(Shaykh ᶜIzz al-Din) and the family of Mand, which ended in the favor of the latter, but the hereditary rights of this North Syrian fief do not seem to have been on a very solid basis."

The Al Shiukh migrated down the Afrine Valley and they claim Mend as their stipulated ancestor. From Minorsky's account he is a Kurd, although not a Yazidi. One of the main Yazidi saints in the area, however, is also named Mend (Lescot, 1938:265-68). There is a Reshkan tribal group among the Yazidi of the Afrine region (Lescot, 1938:110), and the Al Shiukh hesitantly mentioned that they were originally from the Reshwand (Arabic term) tribe (which is called Reshkan in Kurdish) many years ago.

In the seventeenth and eighteenth centuries there were many massacres against the Yazidi. Twenty major ones were counted between 1640 and 1910 (Lescot, 1938:122-25). These forced them into mountain areas or to convert to Sunni Islam. The Land Registration of 1859 particularly encouraged conversion, and many shaykhs who were the primary landowners, tried to maintain their lands through conversion. Those shaykhs who did not convert possessed holdings higher in the mountains. Many landless sharecroppers did not convert. Before 1858, the Yazidi in the Afrine Valley and the neighboring mountain, Jebel Simᶜan, numbered 200,000. When Lescot studied them in 1938 there were 60,000. Jebal Simᶜan bounds the Amik Plain on the east, and the Al Shiukh live near its foothills.

and the political and economic models of the Ottoman period due to modern modification and a period of disruption in the 1930's, these models do help us to understand the general correlation of religious and occupational distributions of people in the region under study. In the Hatay, the *Iltizam* system was prevalent in the cities such as Antakya and surrounding regions; consequently the urban-based bureaucrats and landowners (who were often the same persons or of the same family) were Sunni Muslims of mixed ethnic and linguistic origins, Arabs, Turks, Kurds, Tcherkes, Persians. Many sharecroppers were Nuṣairis, in these regions, while in the mountain regions near the coast control was indirect, and we find cases of landowners who are Nuṣairis. The Nuṣaris are a Shi^{c}i sect and are referred to as ^{c}Alawis.

In the Amik Plain and river valleys leading to it, such as that of the Afrine, the *Iltizam* was officially in operation. Until a century ago, however, the tribes in the area were comparatively free of government control. When the government issued land titles and settled the tribes, many Yazidi landowners of the Afrine Valley converted to Sunni, while the mountain landowners remained Yazidi. Since the Al Shiukh came through the Afrine River Valley to the Amik Plain, this is important in our understanding of their position.

Just as there is a general correlation of ecological areas, social organization and religious identification, likewise there is a general correlation between linguistic and geographical zones. Thus we see that social groups would change their language if they moved to another major ecozone, therefore we have Kurdified Arabs and vice versa, with movement between the plains and the mountains. This has been particularly emphasized recently, due to the association of the modern national state with linguistic identification rather than religious identification.

We will also note in our examination of the area that not only have different political models been present at the same time in a region such as the Hatay, but also various models have operated in the same geographical region at different historical periods. For example, under Roman rule, the Amik Plain was cultivated intensively and widely under the sway of an efficient system of rural administration and taxation operated by an urban bureaucracy. Under most of the Ottoman rule, the same region was used alternately as a winter camp for long-range Turkmen nomads who controlled the area, and by neighboring Kurdish farming mountain groups who planted some of the plain under sharecropping arrangements with the Turkmen and also grazed their herds there.

HISTORICAL AND ECOLOGICAL SETTING   9

   Thus we shall do well to keep these different political modes
in mind when viewing the region and to realize that the constant
changes in administrative borders and the range of control con-
fronted the population with constant choices. It is within this
framework that the alliances and strategies of kinship, marriage
and patron-clientage will be examined as they operate in adapt-
ing to different political alternatives and to the control of resources, both commercial and non-commercial. Keeping these
general principles of organization in mind, let us now look more
specifically first at the general region of the Hatay, and then at
the plain into which the Al Shiukh settled.

ECOLOGY AND THE DISTRIBUTION OF
PEOPLES IN THE HATAY PROVINCE

   The geographical featues of the Hatay are highly varied.
Of its total area, 46 percent is mountainous, 33 percent is plain,
19.1 percent is undulated terrain and 1.3 percent is plateau terrain. The sea coast supports one of the best harbors along the
Levantine coast, and historically it connected the trade routes
from Persia and Baghdad to Europe. Rising off the coast is the
Amanus Mountain Range, a finger of the Taurus Mountains. It
towers up to 7,000 feet and provides a buffer for the Amik Plain
which extends on its eastern side. The plain contains alluvial
soil and is extremely fertile, although agricultural production is
hindered by a lake which expands and contracts seasonally. In
the spring the lake often floods the majority of the alluvial
ground, and in the summer it is scarcely visible. The plain historically has been a locus for trade routes, armies and nomadic
groups, all of which entered through the three major river valleys which lead to the plain. Its population and organization
have not been static. The mountain villages, both of the Amanus
and the other mountain ranges which surround the plain, those of
the Kusair, Jebel A^{c}la and Kurd Dagh, were not threatened or
destroyed as often as those in the plain; however populations
have also moved and been moved in the mountain regions.
   The climate of the Hatay is that of the mild Mediterranean
type, and the annual rainfall shows a great change in intensity
from Antakya for example, which has 44 inches per year, to the
town of Reyhanli only forty miles away in the plains, which has
28 inches. The temperature varies from 19.5 degrees centigrade
average in winter to 28.1 degrees centigrade average in summer.
The rural areas along the Asi (Orontes) River Valley are quite

populated. The villages and estates of the Amik Plain are closer together and contain smaller populations than those of the drier Syrian Plain. Until recently they have been about two to five miles apart with from two to three hundred people. In the wake of the mechanization of cotton production in the area, however, many of the sharecroppers have been forced from the estates in the plain and have settled in slums around the cities. The government, meanwhile, has been attempting to relocate some of these sharecroppers and some populations from northern Turkey in new villages and giving them reclaimed swamp lands to cultivate.

The largest cities in the Hatay are the port city of Iskenderun with 49,000 people and Antakya with 33,500. Antakya is located at the foot of the Kusair Mountains beside the Asi River. It is in a protected position between the Amanus and Kusair Mountain Ranges. The two plains cities of Kirikkhan and Reyhanli have approximately 10,000 inhabitants apiece. Iskenderun has grown very rapidly, and with the addition of a new steel plant to be built by Russia, it is destined to become a rapidly expanding city. The city of Aleppo, fifty miles to the east in Syria, has over half a million inhabitants.

The richness and diversity of the area has provided niches for the different ethnic groups which historically have converged in the area. It has also given the region a characteristic of being self-sufficient, and it has remained partially beyond the reach of full governmental control for much of its history. This was true of its relation to Aleppo before 1939, when the region was part of Syria, and of its relation with Ankara in the present.

Under the Ottoman regime the area was under the administrative control of Aleppo, but maintained a state of semi-autonomy. Economically the area constituted a vital asset for Aleppo, for it contained a seaport and produced much of the fruit and vegetables for the city in the steppe. Historically we even find timber from the Amanus Mountains located in Mesopotamian-Sumerian structures. The Amik Plain provided grain for Aleppo during periods of governmental strength, and during periods of governmental weakness served as a pasture for tribesmen. In its ties to the north, it served as a major trade locus for products going overland to Istanbul and the west. Another economic feature of the area was the involvement of some of its villages in silk production, until the 1920's when the market declined in the whole Levant region.

It is also important to our understanding of the ethnic composition of the Hatay to mention briefly the sequence of recent political events which determined the region's current status. After the disintegration of the Ottoman Empire, through the Armistice of Moudros, October 30, 1918, the Sandjak of Alexandretta was constituted as an administrative unit, and in 1921 it was given a separate administration by the Franklin-Bouillon Agreement between France and Turkey. The Treaty of Lausanne in 1923 did not recognize the Sandjak's autonomy but confirmed the Turko-Syrian boundary fixed through the Franklin-Bouillon Agreement. In 1924 the Sandjak was attached to the new state of Syria under French Mandate.

Turkey did not relinquish its claims to the area. Pre-World War II conditions, including Italy's threats to the Mediterranean, Turkey's control of the Dardanelles and Germany's wish to use them, caused the Hatay to become a pawn in closer French-Turkish relations (see Sanjian, 1956).[8] In 1937, the League of Nations assured the Sandjak of complete independence of internal administration, and bound it to Syria only in the matters of foreign policy (Hourani, 1946:356). In 1939 Turkey officially acquired the Hatay. The position of the Hatay under Turkey obviously increased the control of the Turkish aligned groups over other groups, both in the cities and in the rural areas.

The region forms a meeting ground between four major ethnic blocks. The Turkish speakers predominate to the north and northwest; the Kurdish block occupies the region to the northeast of the Hatay; the Sunni Arabic speakers control areas to the east and southeast; and the Nuṣairis (ᶜAlawis) who are also Arabic-speaking people, have formed a block which is located along the coast and directly south in the mountainous regions of Syria, along the coast. As we mentioned, the wide valleys which

[8]Avedis Sanjian's study of this period shows the use of "ethnic" census material to establish claims to the area. The Arabic-speaking Shiᶜa Nuṣairi were ultimately counted as "Eti Turk" or "Hittite Turk" by the Turkish government. The percentages were recorded as follows: (Sanjian 1956: 39).

Ethnic Groups	Population	Percent
Turks	85,242	(39.0)
Nuṣairi (Arabs)	62,026	(28.0)
Sunni Arabs	22,461	(10.0)
Greek Orthodox (Arabs)	18,051	(8.1)
Armenians	24,911	(11.3)
Kurds	4,831	
Circassians	954	
Jews	474	
Others	130	
Total Arabic speakers	102,538	(46.8)
Total Turkish speakers	85,242	(32.0)
Others		(14.2)

Thus while the Turks represented the most numerous ethnic group, the Arabic-speaking groups actually formed a majority.

lead from these various directions into the Amik Plain have also served as corridors for traders, armies, and the influx of various ethnic groups. The Turkmen came down the valley of the Kara Su River from the north, the Yazidi and Sunni Kurds and the Sunni Arabs live in the Afrine River Valley and the mountains which surround it, and many came from the regions of the north and east. The Nuṣairi Arabs occupied the Asi River Valley and mountain regions bordering it (see Fig. 1).

The major languages spoken in the area are Turkish, Arabic and Kurdish. A few groups speak Tcherkes, and some members of the traditional elite speak French. Previously Armenian and Hebrew were also spoken, but few members of these groups remain in the area. Due to the border characteristics of the area and its repeated shifts in political affiliation, there is much bilingualism in the region. In the rural areas, men tend to speak more languages than women since men are the main traders and leave the villages more often. If a rural woman is bilingual, she has undoubtedly married into a village that speaks a language different from that of her natal village, or she is participating in marketing for some reason or engaged in seasonal labor employment which takes her to different regions.

The major religious communities represented include Sunni Muslims (these are Turkish, Arabic and Kurdish speakers); Shiᶜa Muslims or ᶜAlawis, whose native tongue is Arabic; and a few members of the Greek Orthodox and Judaic faiths (whose native tongue is also Arabic). Ethnically and linguistically the local and traditional upper classes are Sunni Muslims originally of Turkish, Arabic, Persian and Kurdish backgrounds. In general, the Christians of the area before 1939 were merchants and professionals in the urban areas and also lived in villages in the coastal and mountainous regions. The Christian populations also included a significant Armenian-speaking population. These Christian groups were particularly influenced by French culture and learned French during the mandate period. They were also strengthened in their involvement in the silk industry. The upper classes of the Sunni groups, both landlords and bureaucrats, also shared to some extent in the French influence. After the massacres, and particularly when the region became part of the Turkish state, the last of the Armenian community, many Christians and also other Arabic-speaking groups, went to Aleppo and other parts of Syria and Lebanon, while Turkish speakers and other groups began to fill their positions.

Ethnic distribution is a combination of historical, social and geographical factors. A region such as the Hatay is particularly

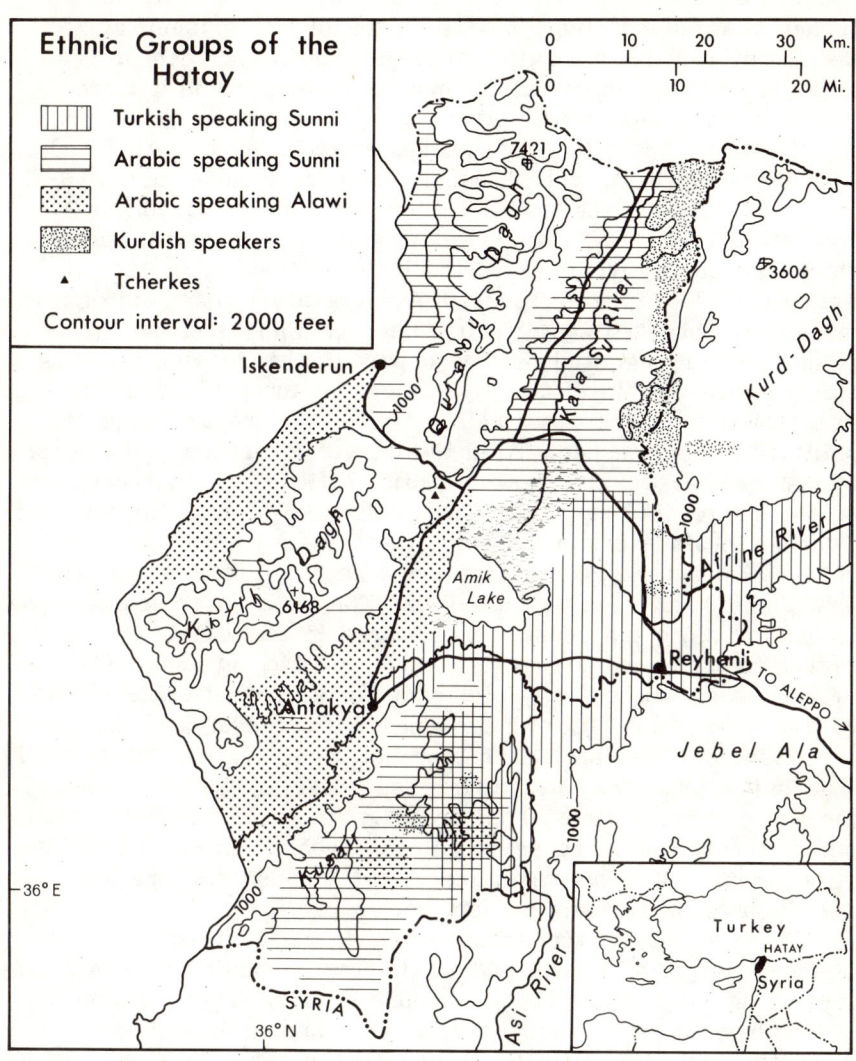

Fig. 1. Ethnic Groups of the Hatay.

complex due to its varied local geography and its location at a corner of different ethnic blocks. I would like to summarize the distribution of the major language groups and then proceed to a very brief mention of the mountain regions and a more thorough discussion of the plain.

The three main language groups in the area are Turkish, Arabic and Kurdish. The Turkish speakers include members of the upper classes, the traditional landed elite, the traditional and new bureaucracy. Historically, some exiled Turkish feudal chiefs (*derebeys*) from the north obtained local importance in Antakya. The Reyhanli Turkmen Confederation consisted of nomads who were settled in their winter camping grounds in the plain a century ago and became a part of the Turkish-speaking ethnic group. Some of the descendents of the noble clans of this confederacy are now wealthy farmers, some are important political leaders, especially in the city of Iskenderun, and some of the members of the weaker tribal sections are sharecroppers on the estates in the plain. There has also been a migration of Turkish-speaking persons from central Turkey who have filled roles as merchants, both large and small, and also some laborers, since 1939. Turkish-speaking villages are also found in the mountains along the coast and scattered in the Kusair mountain region, living among primarily Arabic-speaking groups. These villages seem to be fairly old. Due to the considerable efforts of the government, Turkish has spread since 1939, and many persons know Turkish and another language. This is particularly true in the urban regions, among the upper classes and among the younger generations, both urban and rural. The latter is due to the recent increase in village schools. Most men in the rural areas whose native tongue is not Turkish can speak varying amounts of Turkish, but few women can.

The majority of the Arabic-speaking group in the Hatay are of the Nuṣairi Shi^{c}i faith and inhabit the mountain and river valleys along the coast. This is a portion of a larger area in which they live and which extends from Tripoli in Lebanon, along the Bay of Iskenderun, to the city of Adana in Turkey. Many were sharecroppers under Ottoman landlord rule in the Asi Valley regions near Antakya, but as previously mentioned, retained some autonomy in the more mountainous regions and maintained some portions of land. Recently they have been increasing their ownership of land parcels in the region near Antakya due to numerous factors which have resulted in the decrease of control by urban families. In part it seems to be related to their filling the small craft and merchants' niche in the city, thereby increasing their ability to accumulate cash and also to the increasing interest of sons of landlords in the professions and a decrease in their interest in farming. The positions which the Nuṣairis filled in the urban centers were those vacated primarily by the Armenians and other Christians. A few Nuṣairi have begun to enter the professions. Arabic-speaking Christians in the region are few, but there remain a few villages in the Kusair Mountains and along the coast. Most of those in the city who were engaged in professions and trade went to Aleppo or Latakiya in 1939.

Arabic-speaking Sunni Muslims historically included some urban landowners and also some bureaucrats. Most of these have left the region. There are, however, numerous villagers in the Amik Plain who are native Arabic speakers of the Sunni faith, and who originally came into the region from the Jazira region north and east of Aleppo and from the region of Hama in Syria. These tribal units became medium and small landowners and landless sharecroppers in the southern and eastern portions of the Amik Plain. (These are the societies which are the principal focus of this study.) There are also scattered Sunni Arabic-speaking villages in the Kusair Mountains. In addition, some of the plains and Afrine Valley inhabitants are Arabized Kurds.

Kurdish-speaking groups have existed in the mountain regions on the northeast of the plain since early times; and as we noted, they have occupied the plain during the decay of local dynasties. They also received some lands in the Kusair Mountains, and some of their leaders established soap factories in Antakya and became part of the political elite. In the past we find that recurrent pressures from the northeast sent migrants from Anatolia down into this region. The most recent migrants include the victims of earthquakes, and this has been under the direction of the government. While many Kurds in the plains and in the cities have become Arabized or Turkified, many forgetting Kurdish, those in Kurd Dagh Mountain to the northeast of the plain retain their Kurdish identity and language. An interesting and famous family from this region is the Janbulat. One section of this family currently heads a Druze faction in Lebanon (called Jumblat in Arabic), while another section of the family is prominent in the Ankara parliament in Turkey.[9]

Looking at the mountain and valley populations, we find that

---

[9]This interesting family is discussed by W. Griswold (1966) in his study, *Political Unrest and Rebellion in Anatolia, 1605-1609*.

the Amanus range, which is composed of Kizil Dagh and Gavur Dagh, is not a rich agricultural area, and the villages are widely spaced. There are few large landlords, and most villagers own their own land and are chiefly subsistence producers. Some wood is sold to other regions and the villagers travel to other regions for work, primarily to the richer Kusair mountain area during harvest seasons. The population is Nuṣairi in the south and Turk in the north. In the Kusair Mountain of the Anṣariya range, the slopes absorb water so that the lower areas support animal-herding and the higher regions support olives and grapes. Villages range from 300 to 1000 persons. Kurdish and Arab tax farmers were given fiefs in the region under the Ottomans, and some of their descendents currently represent both large and small landlords.[10] Some lands also belong to families which acquired them through their positions in the urban Ottoman bureaucracy. Some members of the large landowning units moved to Antakya in the nineteenth century, built soap factories and became prominent in politics. The ethnic composition of the Kusair is mixed and includes Turks, Kurds, Arabic-speaking societies of differing religions. In a brief survey, I found that religion defined the endogamous unit rather than linguistic affiliation. Thus Sunni Muslims of Arabic, Kurdish or Turkish affiliation would intermarry, but marriages between Sunni, Shiᶜa or Christian Arabic-speaking groups were few.

The river valley between the Kusair and Amanus and along the riverlets that run into the Asi River are heavily populated areas and are rich in fruit and vegetables. In the past, silk production was important in this region. Much of the land was under the *Iltizam* system and traditionally belonged to urban-based landlords who employed Nuṣairis. Regions somewhat distant from the urban areas and in the foothills of the two mountains were under the *Iqṭaᶜ* and were inhabited by Nuṣairis and Armenians who owned their lands and supported some local elite families.

THE AMIK PLAIN

Early History

Let us consider the history and ecology of the Amik Plain in more length. The region lies at the point where land routes

[10]Turkman estimated in 1937 that 50 percent of the population had no land and worked with a landlord (1937).

diverge in the direction of Egypt, Iran and Constantinople. Early in its historical development, it contained small city-states or kingdoms that fought other city-states, particularly those in the region of Hama, Syria. It then became an important battle area and border region throughout history as both eastern and western empires fought to control it and the river valleys that led to it and which carried the vital trade of the empires. The vulnerability of these trade routes as they passed through the valleys gave the mountain and nomadic peoples an advantage that allowed them to exercise control and use of the valleys and plain whenever the governments could not. During these periods, there existed conflicts between the long-range nomads who passed through the valleys and the transhumants and villagers of the mountains. The Turkmen reported one of the reasons for the creation of a larger confederacy was the ability of the Kurds to ambush them. The three mountain ranges that surround the Amik Plain to the east are Kurd Dagh, inhabited by Kurds, Jebel Sim^can, inhabited by Yazidi Kurds and some Arabs, and Jebel A^cla, which was inhabited by Kurds and Druzes. At the foot of Jebel A^cla, the city of Harim was used by eastern empires to secure the plain.

Large towns and cities such as Antakya and Harim were, for reasons of security, built at the foot of the hills; small centers of trade such as Kirikkhan and Reyhanli in the plain served as caravan stops. Only under stable governments, such as those of the present day, do these small plains trade centers reach the size of a town.

Historically, periods of full-time cultivation alternate with those of nomadic dominance and partial cultivation. Let us briefly recount the settlement of the plain.

In the Assyrian period, the city of the Kingdom of Ungi and strong forts were built through the plain. The plain also hosted a small Armenian kingdom and was one of the areas of Hittite resettlement after the breakdown of the Hittite Empire. During the periods following the destruction of the Armenian kingdoms and after the Assyrian Empire dissolved, Kurdish tribes appear to have occupied the plain. The Greek monarchs, following Alexander the Great, tried to settle these Kurdish tribes when they also established the walled city of Antakya at one end of the plain in 300 B.C.

During the Roman period, the plain and river valleys were well defended by the government; a system of tax farming was established. The area grew grain to supply Antakya, the third largest city in the Roman Empire and its central region of control and recreation in the eastern realm of its occupation. Twice the city of Antakya was captured by Persians, once by Shapur I in A.D. 260, and once by Khosrani I in A.D. 538.

After the Muslim conquest in A.D. 638, Antakya was part of the disputed zone between the Arabs and Byzantium. The latter gained it in 969. Numerous forts guarded it, but it was reoccupied by Muslims who had to cede it to the Crusaders in 1134. In 1149 the Kurdish leader Nur al-Din took the plain, and the great Salah al-Din conquered Antakya in 1188.

Under Ottoman Control

By the time the Ottoman Empire conquered the region during the reign of Sultan Selim (often called Yaguz Selim or Terrible Selim) in the fifteenth century, its organizational capacity was already in decline. The land registers of the sixteenth century, however, contain evidence of settled villages in the Amik; the government had set up tax regions under the Timur system. Transhumants and long-range nomads encroached upon the plain until in the seventeenth and eighteenth centuries. Tribal histories, which I obtained from living descendants and travellers' reports, mention that there were no longer villages in the plains, but only ruined walls which the nomads often used, in combination with their tents, as temporary winter encampments (Volney, 1787; Burckhart, 1822:646).

As the empire met a defeat along the Russian front in the eighteenth century (moreover, when it began to cost more money to keep troops in the field than was obtained through taxation) more pressure for increased taxes was exerted on the tribes. These attempts toward settlement and the state of war along the northern border are mentioned by de Planhol (1959) as factors forcing some of the long-range nomads farther south into the Eastern Taurus and Anti-Taurus, along the border of Syria.

The imperial control weakened further in the early nineteenth century, and nomadic movement and raiding of caravans increased greatly. Some of this movement was initiated and carried out by the government. The confederacies on the borders of government control, initially supported by the administration, now began to turn against the government and consumed the taxes themselves. To control this, the administration moved sections of tribes and gave them military duties in return for land grants in different regions of the empire, thus simultaneously using them as a buffer in weak zones and splitting their

HISTORICAL AND ECOLOGICAL SETTING

home region. The Reyhanli Turkman Confederacy was given land in the Amik Plain in the nineteenth century in such an attempt to settle and control and to obtain taxes and military support.

The forced settlement of groups in the south, such as the Reyhanli, left open a niche for long-range nomadism which was to be filled by Kurdish-speaking groups. The Kurds also were pushed south and found themselves increasingly in contact with Arabs, who were pushing north from the desert due to Wahabite expansion in Arabia itself. These two groups met in the steppe border region of the Jazira, in eastern Syria, and the regions north of Aleppo. Each group was vying for pasture lands, while the government sought to collect taxes and protect its vital trade routes. Pastures of the Jazira were used alternately for summer camps by the Arabs of the desert and as winter camps by the Kurdish transhumants and long-range nomads of the north. Large confederacies, such as the Milli, arose in the foothills which combined Kurdish, Turkish and Arab tribes. Meanwhile, the sheep herders of the steppe region migrated in restricted herding patterns, and those with cattle and sheep followed the Euphrates River areas. The pattern of restricted migration or permanent settlements along a border area would seem to be more logically consistent with the mediating function of members of brotherhoods than would, for example, long-range nomadism. These groups are not as highly ranked as the chiefdoms and remain along the border.

The governmental policy of throwing support alternatively to different factions in these border confederacies and overcrowding pastures often propelled splinter groups (Arab, Kurdish, and Turkish) from the Jazira, migrating in different directions. One of the places for regroupment of these splinter groups was the rich Amik Plain and its adjoining river valleys. Hence the composition of the Reyhanli Confederacy includes Turkish tribes that had been exiled to Rakka, in Syria, and had later found their way to the Amik Plain to join forces with other groups. The Arabic-speaking groups in the Amik today also trace their origins to the Jazira and Urfa regions, as do members of brotherhoods.

Since the Turkmen who took their herds some two hundred and fifty miles north to the Anatolian highlands used the Amik for three winter months only, the Kurds of the mountain regions bordering the plain used the plain in the summer. When the Turkmen were finally settled by the government in the plain and given titles to land there, hostilities between these two groups came to the fore.

The majority of the lands of the plain are now held by absentee Turkmen landlords, while most of the sharecroppers are Arabic-speaking, with some Turkish and Kurdish speakers. Most speak at least some Turkish now. At the end of the nineteenth century in the southern and eastern plain, there were numerous Arab landowners, most of them urban absentee landowners not from tribal background. There are also a few Tcherkes speakers. Tcherkes from the region of Kourban on the Black Sea emigrated to Bulgaria and Roumalia in 1853. At the end of the war of 1877 between Russia and Turkey, they were transported to Anatolia and Syria. At that time they came to the village areas around Reyhanli and Yeni Sehir. In 1931 Jacquot counted approximately 500 Tcherkes (1931:162). Today there are considerably fewer, since most moved to Syria when the Turkish government took control of the region. Many of the Armenians who had survived the massacres of Musa Dagh and Dort-yol were resettled in the plains town of Kirikkhan by Les Services des Refugie du Haut-Commisaire. There were approximately 1000 Gregorian Armenians and 200 Catholic Armenians. All these, however, went to Syria in 1939.[11]

More recent movements of people into and out of the plain include Turkmen from Palestine, who were established in new villages on the plain after the war of 1948. During the past five years, the Turkish government has made an attempt to resettle a group of landless Laz speakers from the Black Sea region. Lands and houses were provided for them from reclaimed swamp lands which the government had formerly rented to Arab sharecroppers in the area. Many Lazs did not stay, however, due to the combined factors of environmental change, unfamiliarity with cotton production (they had previously been fishermen and hillside cultivators), difficulties with the previous cultivators, as well as linguistic and cultural differences. Most rented their lands to the Arab sharecroppers and bought lands in their former villages with the money.

The Amik Plain has thus been an area of resettlement—often by governmental design—as well as a region under the control of large landlords from both tribal and urban background and tenants of tribal origin. Its settlement is far more recent than that of the majority of villages surrounding Antakya and in the mountains. In the past, the conquest of Antakya necessitated control of this plain. When a government was weak, the plain served as a buffer and battleground. In the days of strong governmental control, it supplied Antakya with grains, as it now supplies the cotton factories of the city with cotton.

---

[11] The Arabic name of the plain was ᶜAmuq. In 1938 it was changed to its present Turkish spelling.

II

THE STRUGGLE FOR LAND AND THE ORGANIZATION OF VILLAGES IN THE PLAIN

THE granting of land titles in 1859 and the sedentarization of herding groups in the Amik Plain marked the beginning of the rise of large private estates in that region. Although most of the land remained classified as *miri*, or land belonging to the state, until the twentieth century, in fact these lands were becoming increasingly commercial and patrimonial. The original land system of the Ottoman Empire in the fourteenth century was the prebendal Timar system in which taxes were collected by the Sipahis, or cavalry men, who also obtained their salary from the surplus produce of the villages from which they collected taxes. As we mentioned earlier, in the sixteenth century this system gave way to tax farming whereby these positions were open to bidding. This led to a decentralization in state power and gave rise to a local group of notables called the $^c ayan$. In the mid-nineteenth century, the government made an attempt to reorganize, this time under the influence of western powers, and one of its policies included the introduction of land titles. The intention was to reduce the power of local notables, including those tribal groups which held property corporately, and to obtain taxes. Due to the weakness of the government, however, the result was the opposite, for the existence of small private plots of property only increased the ability of credit-lending notables to obtain the land as collateral from small peasants. It is also important to notice in regard to the Hatay's position in the history of Ottoman land systems, that the empire did not conquer Syria (of which this was a part) until the fifteenth century when the Timar system had already begun to give way to tax farming.

The increasing commercialization of land was an important indication of the spread of the north Atlantic capitalistic cultural system into the Ottoman Empire in the nineteenth century. Increased cashcropping and involvement in increased production for international markets occurred in the twentieth century and was closely followed by European political control. Neither the economic nor political penetration of Europe affected the areas of irregular harvest in northern Syria as intensely nor as early as they did in regions of highly intensive agricultural practices, such as Egypt. However, the region of the Hatay was under French Mandate, and the commercial enterprises, particularly of the silk-producing regions, were noticeable. The highly intensive cashcropping of cotton in the plain, however, has come more recently, in the last twenty years. The capitalistic approach to rural planning since World War II has been influenced by Turkey's close relationship with the United States and such programs as the Marshall Plan and AID. The effects of this system are particularly noticeable in areas such as the Amik and Çukurova plains. These are areas of large, concentrated and level landownings in which there has been rapid stratification and loss of jobs for sharecroppers as machines replaced them. In the past decade several land reform programs have been placed before the Parliament but a major change has not occurred.

Let us go back and look more closely at the early processes of stratification. In the nineteenth century, the second attempt of the government to reassert its authority resulted in the forced sedentarization of long-range nomadic herders in their winter camping grounds. Both the factors of commercialization and sedentarization resulted in an intensive period of economic and social stratification. Members of higher-ranked chiefdom segments became large landowners who engaged as sharecroppers herders of lower rank and persons from surrounding mountain societies with whom they had previously engaged in sharecropping agreements. The settlement intensified the relations of the new settlers with the government and urban markets while it disrupted their previous contracts with the societies which lived in the mountains surrounding the plain. The permanent settlement meant that the settlers kept the majority of the produce of the plain, and most surplus began to go to the urban centers.

Apart from cutting the mountain societies off from their use of grain, the settlement also reduced the ability of these mountain groups to use the plain for their animals, for they let their own animals use the fallow pastures.[1] Numerous conflicts were reported during this period between the societies of the plains and those of the mountains due to this disruption. A spatial change accompanied the social and economic change, for whereas the herders had camped in the foothills surrounding the plain

---

[1] The introduction of mechanized agriculture and use of fertilizer in the early 1950's put an end to the fallow system and almost a complete halt to herding.

during their winter camping period, they settled down on the plains where lands were granted to them. Thus the process created an ecological niche which was soon filled by short-range herders originally from the Euphrates region of northeastern Syria. Many of the members of these tribal sections belonged to religious brotherhoods and served in the role of culture brokers along the boundaries as they have often been reported to do in other regions of the Middle East.

Rank among these short-range herders was not as highly developed as it was among the long-range nomads, and the resulting patterns of village settlement and social organization differed between the two societies. The settlement of the more highly ranked Turkmen chiefdom resulted in the development of an estate system, while the settlement of the more tribal short-range herders developed into a pattern of agnatic core and fringe villages. Although the majority of this study concerns the social organization of the settled short-range herders, their historical development is part of the total process of sedentarization, and we shall therefore give a brief analysis and description of the Turkmen estates in this chapter.

Before looking at each type at more length, we may contrast the types briefly here. When the long-range Turkmen Nomads of the Reyhanli Confederation were forced into permanent settlement, a governmental appointee was designated as the head of the confederacy and individual land titles were given to the notables of some forty clans which composed the confederacy. The notable, on his part, was ultimately subordinate to the head of the confederacy, the Pasha, who was appointed by the governor and was obligated to raise soldiers for wars and collect taxes. After the titles were granted, fighting erupted and the successful notables gained control of larger areas. The nobility continued to live in the villages for approximately sixty years. They granted their descendants portions of the estates, and stone houses were built by this new class. They built mud and straw one-room huts for their sharecroppers, and typically an estate would be comprised of some two hundred of these huts which form a nuclear village, while one or two landlord's stone houses would stand at a short distance from those of the sharecroppers' living area.

Inheritance patterns among the Turkmen followed the general pattern of Middle Eastern rural practices in which sons get equal shares of land while daughters give up their shares (which were equal to half that of their brothers') in order to maintain the protection of their patrilineage. Daughters were compensated in some form by a dowry of mobile property among the Turkish nobility. Due to the commercial nature of the estates, however, members of the family could buy their relatives' shares, and property was consolidated by stronger members, so that corporate lineage groups did not develop in the estate system. The legal change in inheritance rules which Turkey adopted when it changed from the Islamic to Swiss inheritance code of bilateral inheritance in the early twentieth century affected these notables to a greater extent then it did the corporate lineage holders. The transfer of land from one patriline to another through women's inheritances occurred with frequency in the notable class. This seems to be due both to the factors we have just mentioned regarding the commercial nature of land and the lack of lineage corporateness, and to the fact that their previous organization had characteristics of a ramage.

In the nineteen-twenties, sixty years after their settlement, most members of this rural elite moved into the nearby trading centers of Reyhanli and Kirikkhan in the plain, or to the larger urban areas of Antakya and Iskenderun. Currently, the typical landlord's structure on an estate consists of a garage with a few rooms for his personal use when he and his family visit and some sort of structure for his rural supervisor (*wakīl*). The pattern of interaction between the nobility and the sharecroppers is one of a patron and client. Some tribal identity has been maintained by the sharecroppers, however, for it was not uncommon for a sharecropper to change patrons and village residences several times during his life. A sharecropper's tribal connections remained useful strategies in his horizontal mobility when looking for new jobs.

The settlement of the short-range herders, on the other hand, was characterized by different factors, and their village settlement and organization developed into a pattern of agnatic core and fringe villages. These are distinguished by the people as *merkez* (center) and *shoraba* (soup) villages respectively. These herders, as we mentioned, were not ranked as highly as the Turkmen before they settled and were not part of the governmental plan of forced settlement through the granting of land titles. Rather, they entered into the vacated regions surrounding the plain, engaged in a form of contract with both the local plains elites and the mountain chiefs, only later obtaining titles to their lands through political alliances. Serving in an intermediate position between the plains and mountain societies initially and later as intermediaries for urban landlords who were accumulating rural property, we find a pattern of competitive localized agnatic segments which maintained their property corporately

through outside alliances and expanded their control of land into neighboring regions at the expense of other, less successful local agnatic groups. Over the generations, a successful patronymic group forms a highly endogamous and corporate unit while its expansion causes members of weaker groups to migrate, to work their own land, to become sharecroppers or a combination of the latter two patterns. Successful agnatic segments do not engage in agricultural labor but use sharecroppers for this purpose.
The composition of a core or center village, historically included the majority of a strong lineage plus sharecroppers, while that of a fringe village was more heterogeneous, reflecting the processes of expansion by the core into its lands and the acquisition of property by outside groups such as urban landlords to whom the core had aligned itself. Thus the agnatic core maintained its property corporately in the *merkez* village, but property in the fringe villages was owned by various groups. Today, agricultural machinery is being rented and there are fewer sharecroppers in the villages. This is particularly true in the *merkez* villages whose corporateness has enhanced their ability to use machinery effectively. Typical villages are composed of approximately 40 stone houses and a population of approximately 250 persons. There may also be several mud and reed houses for herding and sharecropping families. The *merkez* village may also house a school and mosque.

The cadastral maps drawn some thirty years ago allow us to compare the divisions of a Turkmen estate (Fig. 4) and those of a fringe village (Fig. 3). Figure 4 shows the total divisions of the estate as they have been stabilized through the issuance of a land title during that time. Figure 3 represents the individual plots stabilized within one of some thirty permanent divisions in the fringe village. One may realize the great degree of fragmentation within the fringe village upon noting the different scales of the two maps. The estate is 1/5,000 and the fringe village segment is 1/2,000. Perhaps it is necessary to explain here that within the core and fringe villages there are anywhere from 25-30 permanent sections of the land which never change, and each head of a family has his inheritance scattered so that he has a plot in each of the permanent divisions. Within the fringe village land titles have been issued, and thus the plots are stabilized within the permanent divisions; in the core village these individual plots are changed every year according to a method whereby they draw from a hat for their position within the permanent large sections. We have not included a cadastral map of the core village since it merely contains the diagram of the village

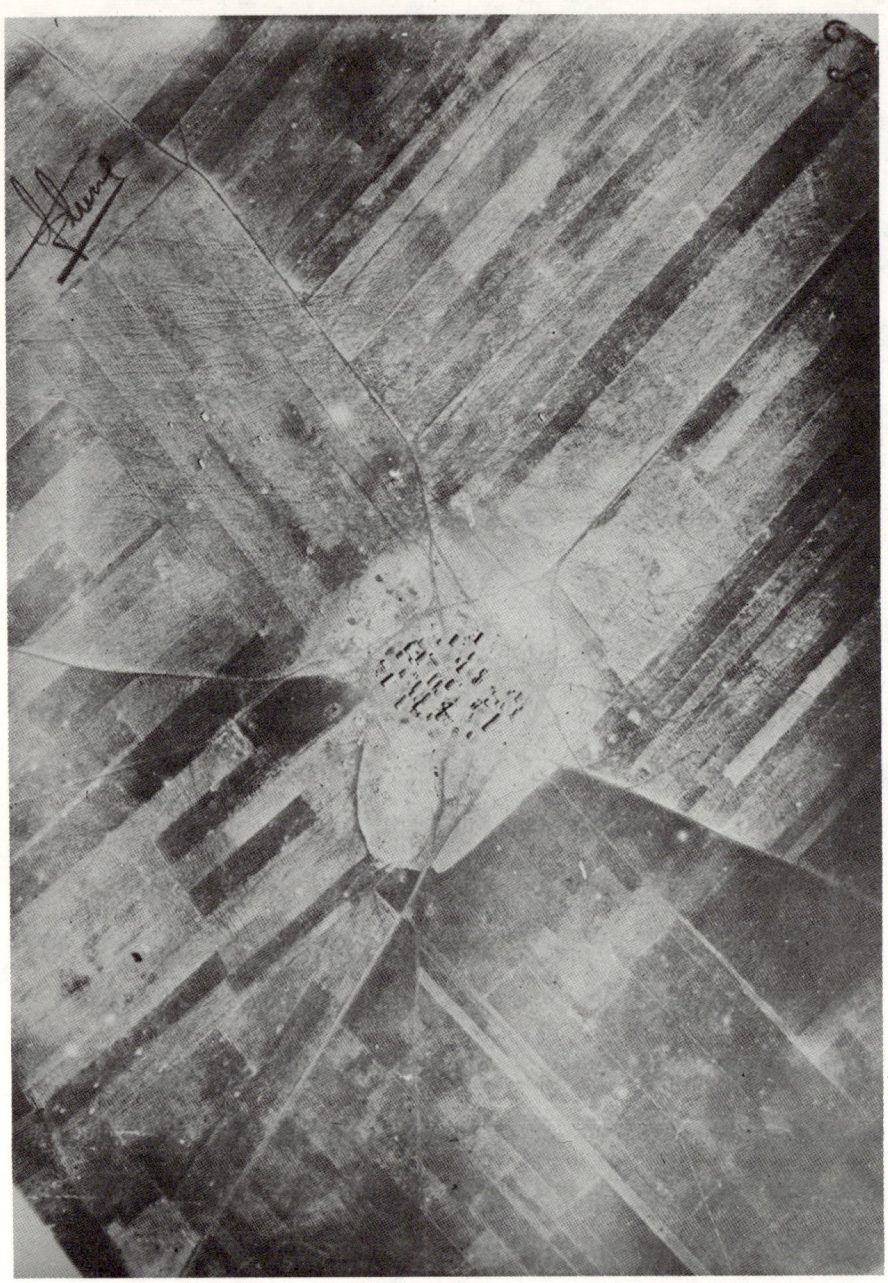

Fig. 2. Areal view of a Nucleated Core Village and its surrounding lands.

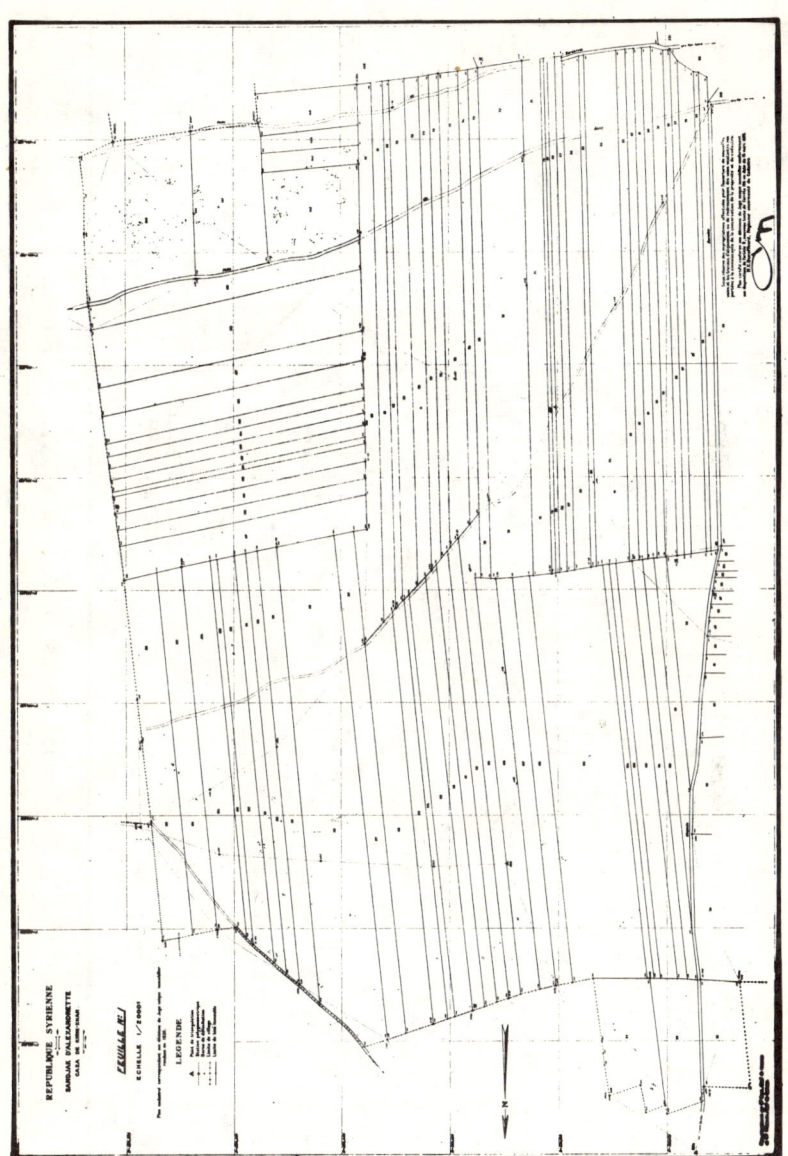

Fig. 3. French Cadastral Map of Stabilized Landholdings in a Fringe Village.

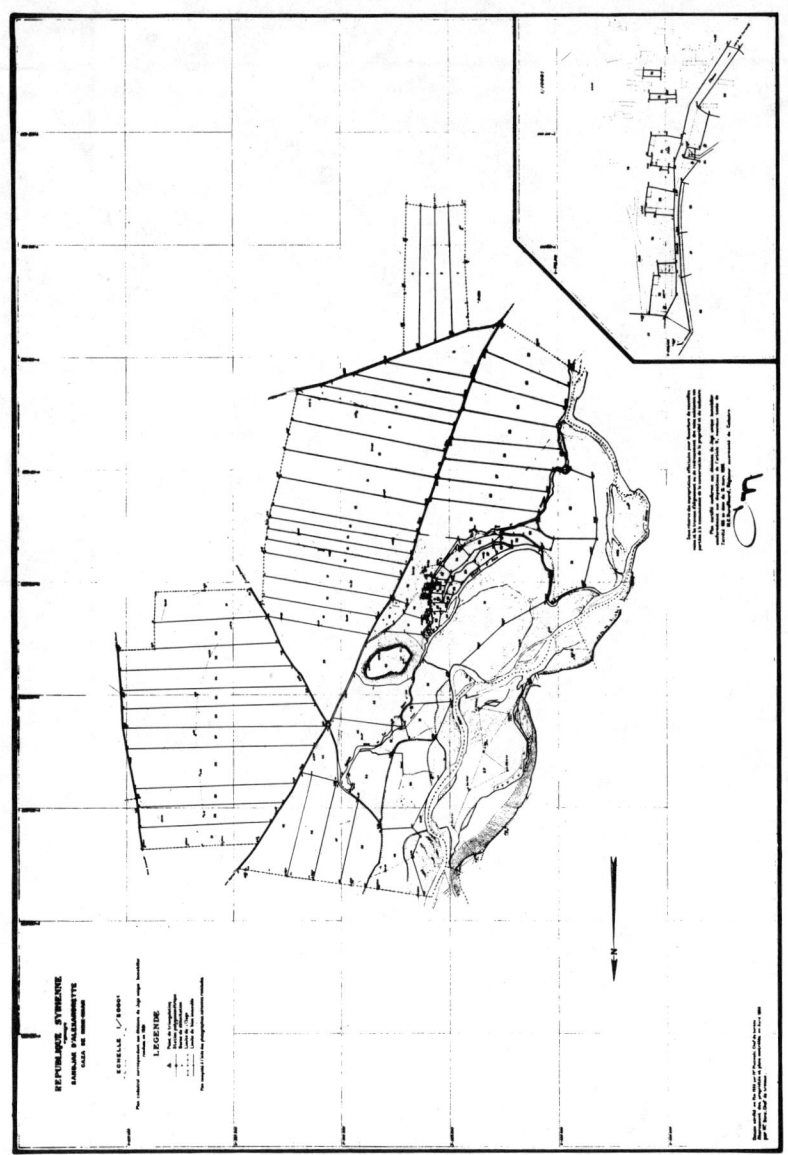

Fig. 4. French Cadastral Map of a Turkman Estate.

LAND STRUGGLE AND VILLAGE ORGANIZATIONS   29

and the exterior boundary of the village lands. We have included however, a photo of a core village which shows the nucleated form of the village and some of its surrounding lands (Fig. 2). Since the period when the photograph and maps were taken, the number of houses has increased and the land has been further subdivided as the population has increased. This further subdivision is also true of the lands of the fringe village, although when a piece becomes absolutely uneconomical, land positions are traded or the land is sold.

In the map of the estate, only the landlord's houses are drawn on the lower right hand corner. These have now been replaced by garage-type structures. The sharecroppers' houses are not represented on the map so I have made a sketch of the distribution of these houses as they appear today (Appendix D). We may add that the term sharecropper is used to indicate anyone who gets a portion of the share of the produce for his labor. On the estates they are usually landless. They are also landless in the core villages. We will find that a steady state of sharecropping to supplement one's own lands, such as Peters found in Lebanon (1963), doesn't occur here in the plain. The processes of stratification in this region of unreliable production have been so rapid that to engage in labor in order to supplement one's crops indicates that one is in the process of losing lands through population pressures or by encroachment by other groups.

Let us now consider each type, the estate and the core-fringe village, more specifically.

TURKMEN SETTLEMENT INTO THE ESTATE SYSTEM

The Reyhanli Confederacy was composed of forty tribal sections that had banded together from various regions to resist increasing tax demands by the government and threats made against their caravans by mountain tribes. It is estimated that nearly 30,000 persons[2] traveled from the Amik to their summer pasture (*uzunyala*) near Sivas in Anatolia, approximately two hundred and fifty miles away. The trip, which began in March, lasted three months; they spent three months in summer pastures and then

---

[2]Burckhardt estimated the strength of various tribes in 1810 as: Serigialar, 500 horsemen; Coudanlut, 600; Cheuslu, 200; Leuklu, 100; Kara Ahmetlu, 150; Kara Solimanlu, 50; Delikanu, 600; Toroun, 60; Bahaderlu, 100; Hallalu, 60; Karken, 20; Aoutshar, 20; Okugu, 50; (1822:634). These are his spellings. Many of these names do not appear today. S. Mursaloglu (Mayor of Iskenderun in 1965) listed the following eight families as important families of the original forty *oymak*: Bahadirli, Löklü, Saricali, Negisli, Kara Ahmetli, Kodali, Coşlu, Kara Sulimanli.

traveled three months back to the Amik where they spent the winter months of December, January and February. In the eighteenth century there was little agriculture in the plains, and what there was was cultivated by members of the villages in the surrounding moutain regions and shared with the Turkmen during the winter months. In terms of agricultural potential, the plain was not supporting as many people as it had in the past eras when it was under intensive cultivation. The Turkmen depended in part upon selling their sheep to Aleppo and Antakya. The traveler, Burckhardt, who visited with the tribes in the early nineteenth century, reported two other economic activities in which they were engaged. He maintained that they transported Arabian camels up to the Armenian area near Sivas where the camels were bred with the stockier Armenian camels. They then brought back the hybrids and sold them for prices higher than those paid for the faster but less sturdy Arabian camel (Burckhardt, 1822: 637). He also reported that they transported wood from the neighboring Kurdish mountains to the Aleppo market on their camels, for the Kurds who cut the wood lacked such transportation (*ibid.*).

Due to the need for strong organization to protect their herds on their long treks, each clan had military retainers. A council was formed of the heads of each tribe. The confederacy was ruled by the descendants of a man whose family was granted a decree from the Sultan appointing him to this position. The family tradition maintains that this decree was given by Murad Pasha IV in the mid-seventeenth century when Mursal Hoca was made governor of the Amik Plain.[3] The Mursaloglu family claims its origin to be Erzurum, and that it was merely placed at the head of the confederacy, and was not a herding family itself. Some of the descendants of the strong lineages dispute the origin and date of the Mursal decree, but agree that the family was appointed by the government. From the Mursal genealogy, one notes that one strong leader after another heads the confederacy generally through the principle of primogeniture. The leader often married many wives at one time, and each wife was a member of an important lineage.

During the seventeenth and eighteenth centuries, we find numerous reports of the government's attempts to stop the confed-

---

[3]The Mursaloglu family's dating is in accord with Burckhardt's, since the latter reports that Haydar Agha Mursal was in control of the region in 1810, and Mursal Hoca preceded Haydar Agha by seven generations. With an average of 25 years in a generation, it would place Mursal Hoca around 1635. The members of the clan that contest this are possibly contesting the effectiveness of the strength of this government-appointed family during the early periods.

eracy from destroying village lands through which its members traveled, as well as reports of government attempts to collect taxes from the confederacy (see Appendix A).[4] Finally, in 1841 a document in the Tapu Defterli (Vol. 36, pp. 295/i, 295/ii, Aleppo, see Appendix A) records the attempt to settle the Reyhanli Confederacy by granting land titles to the head members of each clan section. Included in the same register, land was given to Muhammed Safa Shina, presumably a Kurd from the neighboring mountains. The amount of land given to the individual heads of the lineage was determined by letting a rider ride a horse around as much land as he could in a predetermined period of time. For example, in Tell Gazi four persons were given land; each had fifteen minutes to ride around his piece. Therefore there are in Tell Gazi lands amounting to one hour's worth of riding.[5] This method was described to me by the descendants of the lineages before I found the register which lists the amounts of land in terms of *saat* and *dakika* (hours and minutes).

The herders had originally camped along the foothills surrounding the plain if they were sheep herders, or near the rivers in the plain if they were cattle herders. The lands given to them were in the general area of their traditional camping grounds, although the sheep-herding groups came down onto the plain, leaving some of the hillsides empty. It was, as we mentioned, into this niche that shepherds and cattle herders such as the Al Shiukh moved from the Jazira.

Conflicts broke out immediately after the land grants were given, causing some noble groups to leave the region. Lesser ranked groups entered into sharecropping arrangements with the remaining notables. The increased commercialization of agriculture in the nineteenth and twentieth centuries and most recently the introduction of mechanized farming equipment, furthered the consolidation of property so that today a majority of land in the Amik is controlled by some descendants of the Mursal lineage and some descendants of eight of the original forty tribal sections of the confederacy. The same processes mean that some mem-

---

[4]Orhonlu's and Rafik's translations of early decrees (*firmans*) of the late seventeenth century also show government attempts to settle the nomads in order to protect the caravan routes in Syria and southern Turkey. Semi-nomads, called *konargöçer* were given land and homes in an effort to settle them (Orhanlu, 1963:44-45, 60). They were sometimes excluded from taxes in order to entice them into staying the year round (*ibid.*, 47). Türkman also reports numerous decrees responsible for the exile of Turkmen tribes from the Taurus mountain region into the Rakka and Aleppo area (1937:583).

[5]Among those which the reader could distinguish in this document were: For the Saricali clan, Tell Ghazi, Chatal Huyuk, Taghilghan, Yenijah, Hattabiyeh, Akpinar, Kizilkaya, Baldiran, Murad Pasha, Kirsiz Kuyu, Denan Agha, Kastak, Kizel Koseme; for the Mulla clan, Toursun village; for Kabakli clan, Kurd Nasser village; for Tawakulu clan, Incirli village; for Nour Ali clan, Kayunou Kahda Arali? Kilaal clan, Sohi village; Akgilar clan, Boş Koy; Kara Ahmetli clan, Bardili, Harana, Jefali; Bahirdirli, Kafr?, Awakiya, Tarbilar, Telafi, Musrifiya, Haseneka, Idara, Kadar Aye; Towaki clan, ??. The rest was difficult to read and some of these names are approximations.

bers of these eight noble families also lose property rights and status.

The Turkmen lineages did not hold property corporately then, nor did they act corporately in the political arena. Instead lineage segments vied for alliances with members of the Pasha lineage and with segments of other noble lineages. Close agnates struggled against each other in a manner that seems similar to that described by Barth (1959b) in Swat. This case would also comply with Barth's suggestion that individual land titles and geneological inheritance are correlated with segmentary opposition between brothers and a lack of lineage corporateness (1966). Currently members of the Pasha lineage hold bureaucratic positions and maintain considerable local influence in both of Turkey's predominant parties, and members of the same noble lineage will also be represented in both parties.

Following their political alliances, these noble lineages have traditionally married with the Pasha lineage whenever possible, both giving and receiving wives. They then marry with other noble lineages of the confederacy, as well as with their own close relatives. Men may also marry women of lower ranks, but it is considered a disgrace for women to marry down. In Table 1 we see that the women of one of these noble lineages have married within the tribal section (*Oymak*) more than the men over the last seven generations. As we shall discuss in more detail for the Al Shiukh, the existence of polygyny allows strong units to marry their own women and women of other units simultaneously.

TABLE 1

MARRIAGE PATTERNS OF A TURKMAN LANDLORD LINEAGE
(Seven Generations)

Origin of Spouse	Men's Marriages		Women's Marriages		Men's and Women's	
	%	No.	%	No.	%	No.
Oymak	33	(11)	65	(15)	49	(26)
Non-*Oymak*	67	(20)	35	(8)	51	(28)
	100%		100%		100%	
Within *Oymak*						
FBD/FBS	17	(6)	26	(6)	22	(12)
O.R.*	16	(5)	39	(9)	26	(14)

*O.R.: Other Relative

LAND STRUGGLE AND VILLAGE ORGANIZATIONS 33

If we compare the marriage patterns of one Turkman lineage over a number of generations (Table 1), we find that there are fewer marriages within the patronymic group (ᶜashīret section) than we find for a lineage of the Al Shiukh. The figures are 45 percent and 81 percent respectively.[6]

Barth suggests that there is a significance to the variable of land size in his study of Swat, although he does not elaborate upon it (1965:12). In our case it seems to be a highly important variable in group organization.

Due to the competition between close agnates of the noble Turkmen lineages, tenants also shifted alliances and moved frequently from patron to patron, with consequent splitting of their own kin groupings. The average period of time spent on any one farm over the lifetime of the heads of twenty-nine share-cropping households I interviewed was six years. The landlords were free to expel sharecroppers at any time. Some sharecroppers were armed and served as local guards for noble families, particularly that of the Pasha. The descendants of these guard-peasants are better off economically today than the average sharecropping family. Some of them have obtained land and some bought tractors with loans received through their patrons and are now engaged in hiring themselves out as tractor operators. In return they support their patrons in land disputes.

The past and present pattern of high mobility among sharecroppers on the Turkmen estates is also due in part to the nature of sharecropping, in which the right to work a share is usually inherited by only one son, thus forcing other sons to find work elsewhere, and to the fact that the area is extremely rich and estates are close in proximity. This latter characteristic is in contrast to the Syrian steppe where villages are often separated by many miles. Although the tribal sections (ᶜashīret) of the sharecroppers have insignificant corporate functions economically or politically, and the members are dispersed among many villages, they provide a network of communication regarding opportunities and conditions under various patrons. The sharecroppers have therefore maintained their tribal identification; and it is interesting to note that when the government gave reclaimed swamp lands to some sharecroppers, villages formed on the basis of tribal sections. The government was initially unaware of this since they had previously assigned them Turkish surnames omitting their tribal identification.

[6] The figure for the Al Shiukh is derived from Table 12 and includes all marriages except those to other tribal sections and those made to individuals in town, who are also from other tribal sections. The differences reflect the total environmental situation of the societies and their degree of economic and political corporateness, the Al Shiukh being the more corporate.

Those sharecroppers who came from a tribal lineage that once owned or still owns property retain some form of lineage identity and remain higher in status than those who never held property. All persons of tribal background distinguish themselves from peasants of non-tribal origin, or *ḥāḍarīya*. Although one suspects that some of the *ḥāḍarīya* were originally from a tribal origin, it is significant to note that these distinctions are maintained a century after settlement. Tribal segments have also served as points of entry for the continued movement of herders who become sedentarized.

The composition of sharecropping families on the Turkmen estates varies from one estate to another. On one estate, which I frequented regularly due to its location on one border of my main village of residence, the composition of sharecropping families is heterogeneous in ethnic and social background. The majority are members of Arab or Arabized Kurdish nomadic tribal units who had fled their tribes in Syria. Sharecroppers also include members of landowning lineages from other villages who can no longer live there due either to land fragmentation through inheritance or to their expulsion from fringe villages. In villages farther to the north, the sharecropping families include Turkmen from lesser ranks in the confederacy and a few Kurds from the mountain regions who had previously engaged in sharecropping with the Turkmen when they were using the area as a winter camp. Hence, each estate village may be quite different in ethnic composition, and the majority are heterogeneous due to the mobility of sharecropping families and their landless status.

The Turkmen estate village has no geographic center. Members of the same tribal section often live near one another. But because the houses belong to the landlord, and a newcomer moves into a vacated house, clustering is not always possible (see Appendix D). The relationship between members of a tribal section may be close, such as father and son and first cousins, or distant.

The marriages of the 29 landless sharecropping families interviewed, as shown on Table 2, indicate that 23 out of 36, or 78 percent of the men, took wives outside of the village. This contrasts with Barth's figures of 75 percent village endogamy among a sharecropping non-tribal village in northern Iraq (1953:68).[7] Only 22 percent of the marriages involve relatives within a patronymic unit, and there is little polygyny, with only three men of

[7] The twenty-nine families represent the following diverse tribal sections: nine families from the Mujedma; four from the Na^cim; three from ^cAmirat; six from Jes; one from Tye; three from ^cAdwan; one from Shammar and one Turkish family which acts as the *wakīl*. All these tribal units came from the northern Jazira region and many had been part of the famous border Milli Federation in the nineteenth century which disbanded under government pressures. All speak Arabic, although the ^cAdwan and Na^cim also know Kurdish.

TABLE 2

MARRIAGES OF SHARECROPPING AND WORKING MEN
ON A TURKISH ESTATE

Relationship of Wife	Origin of Wife			Totals	
	Same Village	Same Village Previously	Other Village	No.	%
FBD	3	1			
ᶜAshīret			4		
Total relatives on father's side				8	(22)
Relatives on mother's side			3	3	(9)
Other ᶜashīret (Tribe)	5	1	13		
Ḥādarīya			3		
Total non-relative				25	(69)
Totals	8 (22%)	2 (6%)	23 (72%)	36	(100)

Note–The anthropological abbreviations FBD and FBS will be used to indicate father's brother's daughter and father's brother's son in the text.

thirty-eight having plural wives. One of these men is ninety years old and has had five wives successively. All these marriage figures are in sharp contrast with those found among the Al Shiukh (see Table 3). It is important to note here that although this Turkmen estate is adjacent to the core village of the Al Shiukh, there have been no marriages between members of the Al Shiukh with either the members of the Turkmen notables or with their sharecroppers.

In the past, the occupations of these families consisted primarily of sharecropping, with the landlord providing grain, houses, animals, and the sharecropper receiving one-quarter of the crop after the general tenth was given for taxes to the government. This is the *murāba*ᶜ system (see Appendix C for contract definitions). Other workers included guards and supervisors (*wakīls*). There are still a few sharecroppers, but most are now laborers (ᶜ*amala*) who have jobs related to mechanized agriculture, such as driving tractors or digging irrigation ditches. A few remaining lowly shepherds also live in the village and are exceedingly poor.

Mechanization Effects on Turkmen Estates

Mechanization and cashcropping increased the large landlords' incomes many times over. An interesting comparison of the land production in cotton gives some idea regarding this. When the Turkmen used the plain for their winter quarter and did sharecropping with Kurds, the amount of cotton production a year was estimated at 3.5 kilos per donum. Today with irrigation, fertilizer and machinery, they may obtain as many as 350 kilos per donum per year on alluvial soil of the lower plain. In contrast, with limited use of fertilizer, no irrigation and limited use of agricultural machinery, the Al Shiukh get 45 kilos per donum per year on the *terra rosa* soil of the higher land around the plain.

Mechanization has changed many statuses as sharecropping has been replaced by a system of renting, *Icar* (see Appendix C). Either the landowner must now spend more time in the rural area and become a farmer (*çifçi*), in which case he often builds a rural house for his visits, or he may lease his land to a partner. A new group of entrepeneurs who are leasing land in this fashion are weakening the strength of many of the former notable families. In both cases a manager is employed. The manager will retain the title of *wakīl*; and although his salary is good, due to the high profits associated with the neotechnic system,[8] the rural power and methods of land acquisition which accompanied the position under the sharecropping system no longer exist. It also appeared to me that the *wakīls* are no longer heads of medium-landowning rural lineages as they had been, but are from lower statuses.

As we just mentioned, some descendants of the feudal guards were able to buy tractors and rent them out. They have gained economically and have thus retained some of their power and rural status. (This tendency can be seen in the top income ranges of Village C in Appendix F).

The majority of sharecroppers have been forced to migrate to urban areas or build houses along the roads, for the landlords wanted to cultivate the living areas of the villages. Since the landlords owned the houses, the sharecroppers had no rights. They now engage in seasonal labor whenever possible, and any other job they can find. But even seasonal labor is difficult to find since the landlords can hire mountain villagers at a cheaper

---

[8]See Eric Wolf (1966) for a discussion of neotechnic systems.

rate. There are few industries to absorb the migrating sharecroppers, and they are suffering in the growing slums of the city.

The government has given, sold and rented some reclaimed swamp lands to some of these displaced sharecroppers. Frequent flooding of this land is a problem, however.

The medium income of the twenty-nine families who remained as workers on the Turkmen estate mentioned above is approximately 3,000 TL per year. It is low when compared to the income medians from the landowning core and fringe villages (17,700 TL and 9,000 TL respectively), even in view of the fact that they spend nothing in investment. The children of this village do not attend primary school even though one is located only two kilometers away. They consider themselves lucky to have received jobs on the farm, since most families were forced to leave for the city with nothing when the landowner began to use mechanized equipment. Some of those families that left for the city engaged in cotton-picking and averaged 500 TL per person per season. It requires a family of six to make the equivalent of a farm laborer, and numerous children are desired. The fear that the cotton-picking machines of America will find their way to the Amik was frequently expressed among those dislocated and anxious people.

The sharecroppers and workers of the estates referred to the landowning members of the core and fringe villages as *agha* (landowners of significance), although no urban landlord would do the same. Rural stratification therefore includes the local landlords in the elite category. The *wakīl* ranks next, followed by workers including the tractor drivers, and finally the sharecroppers, followed by the shepherds.

Difficult as the traditional sharecropping system was for the tenant since unreliable crop returns caused him to be in debt constantly to his landlord, still the system permitted him some form of credit. The landlord depended upon him also. Landlords often obtained extra land by aligning sharecroppers on their side of a dispute. The sharecropper could also therefore sell his loyalty and his fighting strength. Now the landlord with his increased wealth depends on machinery; the additional profits accrue primarily to the landlord, secondarily to a group of middle class *wakīls*, renters and tractor drivers, and thirdly to the workers. The workers have little credit, and there is no credit and little work for the majority of the two hundred or more sharecropping families that an estate once supported. The common complaint is that, "Everything is cash now; there is no heart in people. No one helps anyone anymore."

AL SHIUKH SETTLEMENT INTO CORE AND FRINGE VILLAGES

We have mentioned the process whereby the Al Shiukh entered into an intermediate social, economic and geographical position between the plains and mountain communities during the disruptions caused by the permanent settlement of the Turkmen in the plain. We have also said that they did not immediately receive titles to the land, and that their social system can be described as that of competing agnatic patronymic segments in which those who were successful held their land corporately and expanded their control of new lands at the expense of less successful segments, members of which were forced to migrate, to till their own lands, become sharecroppers or some combination of these options. The coalitions which allowed these successful units to expand were made with members of more powerful social segments. A pattern was produced, then, of fairly corporate core villages separated by fringe villages which were not corporate. The granting of titles, the medium socio-political position of the Al Shiukh and the immobility of land seem to be the main factors in the emergence of the patrilineage as a unit which had a high degree of corporateness and became important in strategies of mobility.

Let us view these processes in the example of the Al Shiukh settlement and expansion over the last century in Figure 5 below. The original settlers of the Al Shiukh were two brothers who are represented in the figure as S and O. They had obtained use of portions of border land from settled Turkish notables in exchange for a share of the produce, and they in turn engaged sharecroppers to do the labor. They extended their local power by offering protection against the raids of a mountain Kurdish chief to neighboring agnatic groups similar to themselves (X and Y) in exchange for control of a portion of their lands. Two distant relatives of the brothers, H and J, were then placed on these newly acquired lands, and the four members and their descendants formed a patronymic segment. Marriage within this group by its members has been 83 percent over a period of four and one-half generations. Women have not married outside the group.

The exact nature of their services to the Kurdish chief was not fully explained, but members reported that they exchanged grains and cotton from the plain for soaps, vegetables and cloth from the mountain groups. Their role as middlemen seems obvious.

Returning our attention to Figure 5, we may view the expansion of the patronymic unit in two periods. In Period One, we

LAND STRUGGLE AND VILLAGE ORGANIZATIONS 39

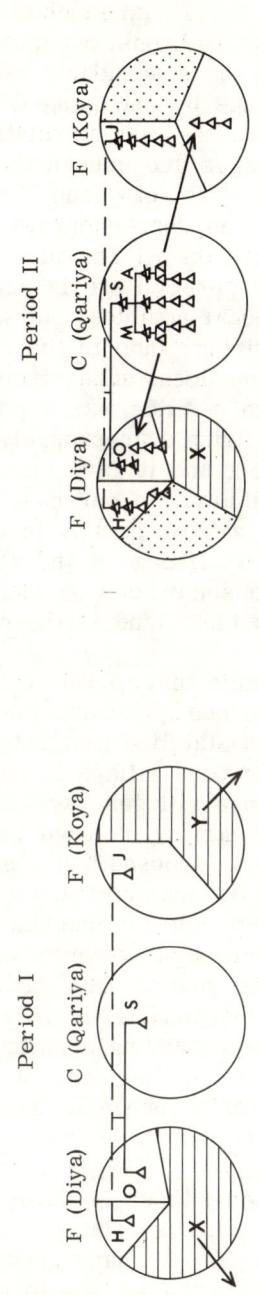

Fig. 5. Patronymic expansion of the Al Shiukh into core and fringe villages: two periods.

Key:
- Property of original patronymic groups living in fringe village areas
- Property of urban landlords
- C Al Shiukh patronymic core village named Qariya
- F Fringe villages of the patronymic core named Diya and Koya

Note: The diagrams represent the amounts of lands acquired by the various groups; however the lands are not compact as shown but rather are scattered in many sections of the villages. The actual number of descendants is not shown, only generations are represented.

see the original settlement and acquisition of land which reflects the simultaneous external alliances with the Turkmen chief and the Kurdish chief. The eldest brother, O, had sons, but those sons had no sons, only daughters, and we find the descendants of S acquiring O's property in the fringe village by marrying O's daughters. It was also in this period that the distant relatives, H and J, obtained land in the fringe villages and caused the departure of members of groups X and Y. Part of group X migrated to Syria and part of group X became sharecroppers with a patronymic unit that is competative with the Al Shiukh.

In Period Two, the expansion by the core village is accomplished not by means of alliances with local notables, but with urban absentee landlords who were acquiring lands in the region. Some of the members of lineage S became local supervisors or *wakīls* on the newly acquired lands. The position was a powerful one locally, since it involved hiring and firing sharecroppers and management over the division of the crop, and it gave new political and economic power to the intermediary. In our case, it also brought acquisition of land from weaker agnatic groups in the fringe villages for both *wakīls* M and A of lineage S and also for the urban landlord. M and A placed some sons on these newly acquired lands and kept others on their land in the core village.

The ability of the core of a patronymic unit to retain its property corporately in the face of numerous governmental attempts to issue individual land titles and stabilize plot rotation is related to these vertical coalitions. The core village has been successful in this attempt, while the fringe villages have not. In the core village, the population has consistently included the majority of descendants of one man and their spouses. It also included a sharecropping lineage, although the majority of this group is now gone, due to the introduction of agricultural machinery. In a fringe village, we find persons of different patronymic affiliations and a changing membership over the years. One such village, Diya, for example, includes some descendants of the original settlers, members of two lineages of the expanding agnatic section which is based in the core village, and a few members of various sharecropping lineages. Also, since absentee urban landlords own property in fringe villages, they may also have their sharecroppers residing in the village.

The vertical alliances mentioned above, those made by the core village people with notables and urban-based landlords, were not accompanied by marriage relationships. We have seen that successful patronymic groups marry within themselves to a high degree. We will show in Chapter Four the method in which those marriages are strategies of mobility. These successful patronymic groups, however, also form a pattern of rivalry and alliances between themselves which is demonstrated through their marriage patterns. The idealized chart below will help us to understand the general strategies among these groups.

First, successful agnatic sections (cores) which are adjacent to each other do not intermarry, rather their alliances leapfrog in the manner of "the enemy of my enemy is my ally." For example, in the diagram below C will marry with C(A) but not with C(R). These are marriages between equals. Another pattern that emerges is that of hypergamous marriages with segments whose lands are being taken by the unit's rival, and in like manner marriages do not exist between an expanding group and the group it is expanding against. That is, C does not marry women of FX or FY, but it will marry women of FC and FD. In these cases the fathers of these women may become sharecroppers of C. Further analysis of these strategies for the Al Shiukh is made in Chapters Three and Four.

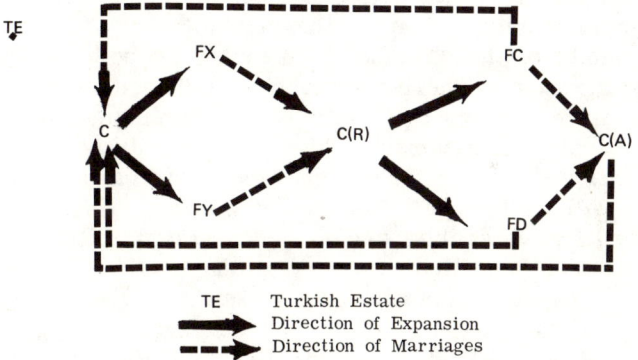

TE   Turkish Estate
→   Direction of Expansion
--▶   Direction of Marriages

Role As Religious Shaykhs

It also seems important here to add some comments regarding the role of the Al Shiukh as middlemen and culture brokers.[9] In their position between the plains and mountain societies during a period of forced sedentarization, their role is clear. They operated in a position of exchange so that some of the products of the plain could still accrue to the mountain people. In addition, they fulfilled the extremely important function of serving as med-

---

[9]For an extremely useful presentation and discussion of the term "broker" in anthropological studies, see E. Wolf (1956).

iators for numerous feuds in the region. Their success and ability to maintain important vertical alliances with the noble families was crucial to their success as shaykhs in the region. Their continued role as shaykhs today is related to their intermediate role between the urban and rural segments of society. Arabic is the common language spoken in these villages of the plains. Most men also know Turkish to some extent, however, women seldom do. The government forbids Arabic to be taught and discourages its use, yet it is commonly used among both the urban and rural lower classes. The shaykhs also have maintained their ability to read and write Arabic over the past 30 years of Turkish rule. This use stems from two factors: (1) their continued role as brokers between a primarily illiterate Arabic-speaking rural population and the urban areas, and (2) as Muslims, command of Arabic is *sine qua non* in a linguistically mixed area.

In addition to their powers of mediation are those of healing. Often these accompany their talents of mediation since expelling the *Jinn*, which is a constant cause of stress and neuroses, often involves using one's reputation for the settling of a dispute.[10] The "psychotic" or accidental cases as they describe them, were sent to another tribal group in the region.

The purity of the shaykhs is inherited by both men and women of the patrilineage. The power to heal and mediate (*baraka*) is passed to them through their stipulated genealogical connection with the Prophet Muhammad. However, inheritance by birth does not make one an effective shaykh. Political and economic power, as well as knowledge of the holy books (which necessitates the ability to read Arabic) and a demonstrated ability to mediate in quarrels are qualities of a strong shaykh. Such a shaykh is then thought capable of many feats of curing. Increasingly important among the qualities of a strong shaykh, however, is his ability to control resources and make effective alliances with urban patrons. The most successful shaykh can then spread his success through bridewealth and loans with little or no interest to his group. Shaykhs also obtain additional income from their healing and mediating services, but a successful shaykh charges little and now receives his wealth through secular means.

---

[10]The methods of their treatment include the use of steam and message, principles basic to physical therapy today. Tiles are boiled in a large pot while the head shaykh and the patient stand over the pot with a sheet over their heads and the shaykh massages the head of the patient. Meanwhile, pieces of paper on which proverbs from the Qur'an are written are put into the pot, and the head shaykh recites similar proverbs. The patient must stay in the shaykh's house for three days and three nights and receive this treatment every night. At the end, he is hit in the face with a shoe three times. I found this same process mentioned in legends of the Kusair Mountain saints of Kurdish origin.

Mushāʿa Tenure

Since it is not only shaykhly lineages which own property corporately, and since there has been some discussion regarding what has been termed *mushāʿa* (shared) ownership in the Middle East, perhaps we might add a few comments on the subject at this point.

First it may be noted that *mushāʿa* property is not described in regions of intense irrigation such as Egypt, nor in intensively cultivated mountain regions such as Lebanon. Rather, we find it in the plains regions such as Syria, which are characterized by unreliable rainfall and harvests. These regions have also been under the alternating pressures from nomadic and urban sectors.

In the literature, the term *mushāʿa* has been used to describe quite different patterns of land holding. For example, Post (1891) used it to designate ownership in which land was redistributed to villages according to ". . . their ability to cultivate, their standards being the number and power of the cattle used for plowing" (1891:105). There is no mention of whether these are relatives, and thus it seems that the village boundary delineates the corporate group, not kinship. In our case, distribution of the rights of usufruct is determined by genealogical reckoning according to the general pattern of equal shares for sons, and the boundaries of the village contain the majority of the lineage. Administrators regard both forms as *mushāʿa* property, but there is an important difference. Barth mentions that equal redivision occurs among Kurdish lineages according to the number of living men in the lineage. This is another type of redivision. Unfortunately, neither of these two studies gives examples of these processes of equal division among living men disregarding genealogical reckoning. Among our villages, the areas are reallotted by a drawing of position from a box, but the amounts are not equalized in that fashion, they are derived through rules of inheritance.

The term *mushāʿa* was not one of the legal land classifications of the Ottoman, nor of later regimes. In our case, the lands were originally prebendal, or *mīrī*, lands belonging to the state, and later one title was obtained and rights maintained for descendants of the settler. It is interesting to note that the villagers themselves do not use the term *mushāʿa* to refer to their method of corporate ownership, but when it is used it refers to a region of rocky lands which is shared by two or more villages and on which they graze their herds.

We have mentioned the techniques of land registration by which various governments have attempted to obtain control of peasant surpluses, and how these have resulted in the rise of a credit-lending landowning elite. Throughout our study we shall see how the agnatic corporate core village has been able to acquire advantages, politically and economically, over the heterogeneous fringe villages during this process.

Researchers have attributed collective ownership to the nomadic origins of villagers in the Levant; others have viewed it as a result of feudalism. In this study, the case is not so easily dichotomized. Corporate ownership among the Al Shiukh has been seen as continuing the tribal custom of a common tribal grazing region. However, the custom operates within the new framework, that characterized by immobile property in a period of stratification and commercialization of the nineteenth and twentieth centuries. It serves as a mechanism for expansion and upward mobility as well as a defensive strategy against urban forces of power.

Physical Appearance of the Villages

Physically the core and fringe villages resemble each other and differ considerably from those of the Turkmen estates. The villages contain 40 to 50 long, rectangular stone houses with red tile roofs. Most face the same direction so that the wind which crosses the area strikes only one smaller side of the house. Each house has two rectangular rooms placed side by side. One room is used for guests during the daytime and as a sleeping room at night. The other is used for household duties such as sewing and preparing food. The houses differ minimally in size or appearance. If the family is polygynous, one wife and her children will occupy each room; and in some cases, if there are more than two wives, a smaller one-room separate house will be built. Brothers live next to brothers, and in one core village, there are compounds in which all the male descendants of each of the original settlers' wives live. These divisions are not noticeable with the eye. In the fringe villages, the different patronymic and lineage segments live in different sections of the village, but again this is difficult to observe. Each tribal section also has compounds similar to those in the core villages. There is no visible center to these villages, and as we mentioned, houses are parallel to each other. In the vicinity of each stone house, and sometimes attached to it, is another rectangular house made of mud bricks. These structures once served as houses for sharecroppers and now serve as sheep houses. No walls connect any of the houses. These settlement patterns are quite different from other plains villages reported, for example, in Tell Toqaan in Syria (L. Sweet, 1960) and reflect, it seems, a camping settlement of herding people.

Although the houses are all a similar shape and size, the composition of kin groups living in them varies and may include a nuclear, polygynous, or a variety of expanded families. The separate household is also not necessarily a separate economic unit, for the extended family remains the basic economic unit as long as the father is alive and able to maintain unity in the family. Some portion of his inheritance is customarily given to a son temporarily, but it is often only enough for his food. The father may have more sons later on, and it is easier to add to a son's inheritance than take it away in the final period of division.

Within each village there is a guest room (*oda*) which is always the home of the strong man in the village. It is sometimes larger than the average guest room, and traditionally was larger than it is today. The room is generally reserved for the men of the village, and women seldom are seen there. Whenever there is a guest, all the men come to pay their respects; and in general much time is spent in that room discussing politics. These groups have much leisure time since they do little physical labor and the days and evenings of winter are long. The battery radio is a necessity, and five major international stations are listened to regularly. The range and depth of comprehension of international politics greatly amazed me. For example, names and voting records of several American senators were known and discussed.

The guest room of the Al Shiukh is also used for groups to gather who come to the shaykhs for the settlement of a dispute or to be healed. Guests who come from a distance stay overnight and are always fed by the head shaykh and mediator. Small fees are received for acts of healing. The floors are covered with brightly woven rugs and there are many cushions in the guest rooms. Nargilas and coffee-making utensils are kept cleaned and ready for use.

III

PATTERNS OF DESCENT, INHERITANCE AND MARRIAGE AMONG THE AL SHIUKH

DESCENT AND INHERITANCE RULES

WE have discussed the conditions of sedentarization, the issuance of individual land titles and increased market involvement which constitute the general ecological background for the rise of landholding and landless groups and their variation in organization. We have indicated that, in general, the nature of organization of kinship and strategies of mobility is related to the relative amount of land obtained during the nineteenth century, which in turn is related to the rank of the societies before sedentarization. We found that large landowning lineages with individual titles to portions of land were not corporate; and that their horizontal alliances as matched by their marriage patterns were more ambilateral, operating within a political moiety which was controlled by a state-supported Pasha lineage to which they were related in a system of political and marital relations. They related to landless sharecropping groups through a system of patron-client relations devoid of kin relations, and to certain intermediaries through hypergamous marriage patterns. We also found that landless groups retain tribal affiliation but that this affiliation is not organized around a corporate estate, and few marriage alliances exist between close kin. Rather, the tribal affiliation is one means of obtaining communication in regard to new jobs and thus to physical mobility, and these are similar in function, and supplement strategies of marriage which are normally to units outside their kin group. Finally, we have found that it is the intermediate societies, i.e. those with medium landholdings and who serve as intermediaries, who emphasize general kin group corporateness the most, both in terms of controlling land and in terms of making intra-group alliances through marriages. These societies also maintain non-kin vertical alliances to higher ranking social segments. Marriages to women of lower ranked groups

often accompany patron-client relationships which involve sharecropping contracts with the father or brother of the woman.
Since descent is patrilineal, the lower status of the wife in this case would not reflect upon the children of the union.

All these groups just mentioned maintain a similar general ideology of patrilineal descent, but it is the class and total ecological situation which determines the composition and organization of groups and alliances as they operate within this ideological framework.

In this chapter we shall discuss formal kin terms, the rules of descent and inheritance and the transfer of bridewealth among the intermediate society of the Al Shiukh. We shall also discuss their marriage patterns in relationship to and comparison with other socio-economic groups in the area. In the following chapter, Chapter Four, we shall study the patterns of strategies and alliances, kin and non-kin, among the Al Shiukh from a diachronic viewpoint over four and one-half generations, that is, from the period of their initial settlement in the area to the present. We may precede the analysis by stating that the material presents us with a system that is patrilineal in integration as well as patrilineal in ideology. Kazdan and Murphy have argued that a system with a pattern of FBD marriages is an endogamous society and that its patterns of integration must be bilateral.
They also see an endogamous system as one that operates mainly toward fission and the encystment of units. We will find that although this society has as high a rate of marriages within the patryonymic unit as I have seen recorded, it simultaneously has important alliances outside the group; and thus one cannot refer to the groups as endogamous. Second, we find through an analysis of their marriage alliances that the patrilineage contains divisions, and yet the majority of it obtains a degree of corporateness and continuity if viewed during a process of expansion. Basic to our disagreement, then, is the fact that they have used a mechanical model, not a dynamic one; they have also neglected polygyny, a very important factor in the method whereby an expanding unit does not encyst itself. Also there is the fact that those authors have failed to make the distinction between the juxtaposition of persons on the ground, and the principle of descent as it operates in a framework of political and social strategies. They feel that through endogamy, persons of the group have the same grandparents through their father's and mother's side. This, of course, is not a characteristic of other groups that have been described as bilateral, and the lack of strict endogamy means that few meet this requirement anyway. In this respect, I agree with Marshall

Sahlins when he states, "Descent is not recruitment, but arrangement and alignment, in the first place a principle of political design." (1965:105)

We may mention another point before we begin a description of marriages and descent, and that concerns the patterns of alignment. They differ from those found in Africa, where close collateral segments align against distant ones. And they also differ from the pattern which Barth found among the Pathans and which is more characteristic of the large landowning Turkmen, in which close agnatic collateral segments align with distant ones against each other (Barth, 1959b). Rather, among this intermediate society, we find that both the main opposition and alignment occur simultaneously among the closest agnatic collateral segments at the center of a patronymic kin group.

I would like to comment that through a dynamic approach to the discussion of alliances and viewing them in their total ecological perspective, I am struck by the general similarities to those processes and patterns of strategies of mobility among different socio-economic groups in Ecuador which were recently discussed by Whitten (1969). There are also numerous similarities to Peters' discussion of rank and marriage in Lebanon among the Shi^{c}is (1963). However, due to the proximity of the areas of study, the differences between our two studies are also interesting. In the village which Peters studied, land is regularly alienated from the agnatic group by women whose inheritance is equal to that of men. There is also a middle peasantry in the village he describes, that is, a peasantry which owns its lands and works them while simultaneously working the lands of an elite for a share of the product. In the Amik Plain, as I mentioned, we find few members of this middle peasantry, and most sharecroppers are landless or are in the process of becoming that way.

Kinship Terminology

The terms used to identify the formal kin groups must be viewed as functions of the dynamic nature of kinship; hence the terms include no groups definable as to their exact composition. Evidence of this statement is seen in the disagreement among members regarding the persons to be included in these groups. This is principally due to the fact that the terms are partially political in nature and partially genealogical. Genealogical segments of the same depth are not equal in strength and do not operate in equal patterns, therefore we find the same term used for groups of differing composition.

The primary group of identification within the area is the localized tribal section which is composed of lineages related either in fact or in fiction. Such a unit carries its tribal name (ᶜashīret name) and is usually represented in several villages. Societies in other regions of the Middle East use the term *hamūla* for such localized descent groups, but sedentarized nomads in this region do not. When asked to give an example of a *hamūla*, the Al Shiukh most frequently mention an urban notable family. The word *familia* is given as also being correct, but it is never heard in use. This word is a Kurdish word of the Sulaimaniya dialect and seems to have borrowed from Persian (personal communication from Dr. Ernest McCarus, Ann Arbor, Michigan, 1969.)

Divisions of the ᶜashīret section receive patronymic appellations. The first encountered is "the children of so and so," the latter being the original settler in whose name the lineage land title is made. A second unit that carries a patronymic title is ideally a three-generation unit called an *'ahl*. This unit is important for it contains the contemporary leader of the ᶜashīret section as well as his primary opponent, and the major processes of lineage fusion and fission occur within this span of the central core. These patronymic groups can only be understood in reference to the segmentary processes since the genealogical composition varies according to the strength of the segment. Thus an *'ahl* peripheral to the major center of lineage control might include four or five generations. For the purpose of identification to persons outside of the region of local politics, a member will give his first name followed by his father's name and then his ᶜashīret name.

A political faction is called a *fakhidh* (division) among the Al Shiukh. Thus, a named group is only relevant if it includes a period of historical or temporal element. It will be remembered that the initial settlement of the Al Shiukh included members representing different *fakhidhs*. "Brother" was used in a classificatory sense between members of the same *fakhidh*, while "cousin" was used between members of related *fakhidhs*. These former divisions are now meaningless in current political alliances. Among nomadic herders, a *fakhidh* can separate physically and move apart, but in sedentarized groups, a *fakhidh* covers several villages as lineages expand.

Among the Al Shiukh shaykhs, long demonstrated genealogies are not common; four and five generations is the rule. Since they rely upon their religious castelike organization for status, they do not trace their secular genealogies extensively for they

DESCENT, INHERITANCE AND MARRIAGE PATTERNS

might show alliances which they do not care to have known. Part of their strength as saints and mediators lies in their neutrality and comparative freedom from warfare with outside groups. Instead, they stress their mythological and universal genealogy. As a case in point, it was only after a year that they finally informed me that long ago their ancestors came from the Reshwand tribe, which appears to be the Reshkan Kurdish tribe. Since they consider themselves of Arabic derivation, and their native tongue is Arabic, this information confuses this affiliation and in addition does not aid their current position as Turkish citizens. In contrast with the information given by the Turkmen regarding their genealogies, the shaykhs were able to mention all the marriages of both men and women within five generations. The task of remembering women's marriages is made simpler by the fact that successful shakhly lineages such as the Al Shiukh do not marry their women except to close relatives. More important, however, is the political and economic nature of marriages and the involvement of members in these alliances.

In contrast, we may note that the leading lineage of the secular Reyhanli Turkman Confederation dates back three centuries, or eleven generations, and one of the Confederation's noble families, eight generations. Certain members are omitted and beyond five generations, the latter noble lineage includes only one son a generation. In general, women's marriages are remembered with less accuracy or are supressed, particularly if they happen to have married into a lineage segment that had since decreased in power. If women marry into a higher ranked lineage, they are, of course, always remembered.

Barth mentions that in areas where there are written genealogies, the conscious reorganization of genealogies to fit the social facts is more difficult (1965:25). Although this may be true in part, it would appear that in the Middle East, rather than slowing such a reorganization, it merely increases the area for dispute. The Turkmen aristocracy constantly disputed each other's claims. The urban landlords easily insert famous personalities such as Harun al-Rashid and Abdulqadir Jilani into their genealogies to justify their noble status. Among the Al Shiukh, knowledge of actual relationships does not stop them from using classificatory terminology to identify social distance. Hence written genealogies and histories are more fuel for disputes if so desired. Persons can be and are taken off and added onto the written records, as records are rewritten. These claims then are only valid if the members are strong enough or interest enough to enforce them.

As one would expect, genealogies of sharecroppers become

less precise, particularly concerning the marriages of women of their lineages. This is understandable since most women marry outside of the kinship group. Sharecropping lineages are spread among many villages, inheritance is minimal, and since descent groups have few functions, it is difficult to keep account of all the members. Although the preceding statements are generally valid for most sharecroppers, if a landlord has recently acquired the lands of a village, patrilineal groups will persist until individual contracts and forced migration result in the formation of the stem family. The degree, then, to which lineage groups decline in their importance among sharecroppers depends upon the length of time in which the lineage has been engaged in sharecropping. On the other hand, the reverse process was also noted in the Amik Plain. New villages composed of members of tribal sections promptly regrouped when given land under a governmental project of land reclamation. As I mentioned, there were lineages that had been dispersed for almost a century, and they organized into patterns which seem similar to other landowning groups in the area. These kinships patterns were not evident to outsiders at first, because distinct Turkish surnames had been substituted by the government for tribal names. The dispersed nature of sharecropping alliances is also evident in the fact that one has to ask numerous members of a lineage about marriages and relations in order to complete genealogies; few know them well. Among the landowning Al Shiukh all members, both men and women, can outline all the marriages of their lineage over five generations.

This knowledge among the Al Shiukh is related to their high degree of endogamous marriages and the economic transfers that accompany the marriage and inheritance patterns. Descent, however, is reckoned strictly in the male line. The emphasis upon demonstrated agnatic descent increases as the degree of sedentarization increases. Due to this emphasis, we will be concerned with patrilineal segments in much of this analysis. The accretion of other patrilineages through a linking marriage in which a woman of a lower group marries a man of a strong lineage, as we find in the process of alliance formation in nomadic society (Peters, 1960:41), does not take place once sedentarization has occurred. These latter types of relationships evolve into patron-client relations between landlord and sharecropper.

Only persons of a lineage are entitled to a share in the property once the title is acquired. All sons, regardless of their mother's origin, get an equal share in the corporately owned patrimonial land. In one study of a nomadic society in the Middle East, on the other hand, it is reported that "males of impeccable patrilineal descent but from a mother of low caste, may be considered tainted by their mother's low status and denied a share in the section's estate" (Pehrson, 1966:19). In the case of a man among the Al Shiukh who has no sons, one-half of his land passes through his daughters to their sons, while the other half is transmitted to the deceased's full brothers or full brothers' sons. Thus in some cases sons inherit from their mother also. Since such propertied women are always married to close cousins, and since there is polygyny, inheritance through mothers consistently is maintained within a close patrilineal segment but also often creates a differential amount of land control between half siblings.

By Qur'anic law, a woman is allowed one-half of the amount of inheritance allotted to her brother. Under modern Turkish inheritance laws, taken from the Swiss Code, a woman gets a share equal to that of her brother. However, in the Al Shiukh villages she will never claim it. Instead, she gives it up in return for the protection which her father and brothers offer her. To acquire her inheritance means a dependence upon her affinal family and causes much insecurity, according to the women of the village. That this occurs in a society such as the Al Shiukh, in which all the women marry within their own patrilineage or related lineages, discredits a hypothesis put forward by Murphy and Kasdan that parallel cousin marriage and endogamy produce a system in which there are no mechanisms "for the maintenance of structural balance between consanguinal and affinal relatives."[1] By relinquishing their rights to one-half a brother's share of property, women of the Al Shiukh retain rights in their patrilineages and are never completely absorbed into their affinal family, except when they are widowed and substitute in the role of their deceased husband. We will turn to this latter situation in a moment.

Possibly due to the frequency of polygamous unions, in five generations only two men of the lineage have died without sons. Seven daughters were involved in the two cases, and each was married to a powerful close agnate (see Figs. 7 and 8). A propertied wife may be in a favored position with her husband, but in reality the passing of property through her is a guarantee that a brotherless girl will get protection equal to that of wives who have brothers to protect their interests. Needless to say, a woman living closer to her family or from a strong lineage need

[1] Murphy and Kasdan, 1959:25.

not be as apprehensive for her security as a girl from a lower ranked group or a girl who lives a considerable distance from her natal home.

Among other rights which a woman maintains in her patrilineage are those of aid and protection. Although she has no right to abandon her husband, if she is treated badly she freely returns home if it is nearby, and her father or brothers negotiate for her with her husband's family. Divorce seems to vary greatly among societies in the Middle East. Among the Al Shiukh there has only been one divorce in four generations, and that was due to unusual health circumstances. Therefore, in reality the men have no more rights in divorce than the women of this group.

Just as her family is responsible for providing aid for a woman, it is that family which she dishonors by bad behavior, and they are responsible for her punishment. The ultimate punishment is in a case of adultery or premarital intercourse and by tribal custom is death. This threat is more rigidly applied to women of noble and landowning lineages. Cases were revealed to me in which a landowner impregnated a woman of a client sharecropping lineage, and she was not married to him until after the birth of the child. With the desire for such a marriage, she was not punished by her family. Yet another tells of a man who shot his pregnant wife for alleged infidelity. She was from an unrelated tribe which lived in a different region.

The fact that the sister's brideprice is often used to gain a wife for her brother increases the brother-sister bond, and the common occurrence of brother-sister exchanges in marriage furthers this close relationship with her lineage. In a polygamous household, the full brother and sister are closer, and sibling exchanges are attempted between full brothers and sisters before those exchanges which involve half-siblings.

In the case of the death of a man before his sons are mature, control of the property passes to the deceased's closest male agnates. If his widow is a member of the patrilineage, however, she gains control of the land when her son reaches approximately twelve years of age. She then moves back to her husband's home, taking any other wives of her husband and their children with her. She manages the land and works within his system of alliances, not those of her brothers. In these cases the widow never remarries, and the property is controlled in her son's name not her own. Her co-wives also will not marry, but will reside temporarily with their own or their husband's brothers until the unit recombines.

DESCENT, INHERITANCE AND MARRIAGE PATTERNS

A widow with only daughters cannot perform such a substitution role, and neither can a woman from outside the lineage. These prohibitions are for different reasons. If there are sons, the woman is helping to preserve the segmental nature between close agnates; she is substituting for her husband and his son. If she remarried, it would be in the levirate; it would combine two segments which are potentially oppositional segments, those between closest agnates. In the case that a sole widow has only daughters, the segment has already been extinguished, and she will usually marry in the levirate. If she is from outside the lineage, there is too much danger in trusting an outsider in the job of property control even in the name of her son; thus the trust is given to the father's brother until the son is of age. There are many combinations. For example, there is a case in which one man's widow is a member of the lineage and has a son, and another of his widow's has only daughters. Neither married, and when the son was of age, they became an economic unit with the widow who has a son heading the unit and substituting for her husband. There is also the case in which an unmarried elder sister took over control and raised her full brothers, remaining the head of the household even after the maturity of her brothers.

Several such cases were found in the land history of the Al Shiukh (see Aswad, 1967). Such a woman becomes a substitute for her husband and essentially has the power of a man, except in her ability to contract major patron-client relations with urban patrons, merchants and landlords. The increased involvement of the villages in cashcropping has decreased women's chances for positions of power due to the predominance of men in important merchant roles in the Middle East. Some widows of the village readily and angrily point this out. Within the community, however, and with her kinsmen and sharecroppers, she can arrange contracts freely. The function is to maintain distinct and close patrilineal segments within the larger patrilineage, since it is between brothers that competition for leadership of the lineage occurs. This process will be outlined in the next chapter.

It is important to note that the property passed through a woman without brothers goes only to her sons; it does not become part of the husband's land which would be divided among all his sons and would include sons from other wives. A husband may act as a steward for the land if his wife's father has died; in cases where the father has not died, the husband may never get a chance to control it at all. This principle of inheritance reinforces the principle of the "unity of the womb" which relates to the factional struggle between close agnates. One of the most common points of lineage fissioning is between half brothers, this occurs regardless of the origin of the mothers or whether the mothers are propertied or not. The difference in inheritance obtained from a propertied mother results in an economic inequality between sets of half siblings. Among the Al Shiukh, it has resulted in differences between nine out of nineteen sets of half siblings in four generations. Even though some property may on occasion pass through women from one patrilineal segment to another, married women primarily serve to divide sections in the system of competing close agnatic segments. Thus half siblings may be identified by their mother's name at times, but as Daghestani has mentioned, this identification serves to distinguish males united through a mother; the identification is to her and not her family (1932:164). This is merely a means of identifying a patrilineal segment which is important in oppositional alliance and is retained only for a generation.

Sons get little if any property until their father dies. A man's son may die at the age of fifty without ever receiving his total inheritance. Several such cases occurred in the history of this lineage. The long life of a father tempers the tendency toward primogeniture, and the elder sons spend more years without their rightful share than the younger brothers. The father gives them only a small portion of their share. Conversely, if a father dies young, the case for primogeniture is strengthened, particularly in the case of a polygamous household in which there may be considerable age difference among his sons who are half brothers.

In cases where a father has accumulated debts, the brothers will pay off the debt first and then divide the land. Economically, then, the family is basically an extended family, although in residence patterns sons live in separate structures after marriage. These structures are next to each other; thus within the village, residence patterns are patriunilocal. The youngest son and his wife remain with the father and inherit his home.

One of the most important portions of inheritance is the provision of a house at the time of the marriage of a son. If no house is available, and if the wife's parents do not persist in demanding a new structure, the son and his wife may live temporarily with the father, but it is considered somewhat of a disgrace. In the period when sharecroppers lived in the village, their houses adjoined each home of the Al Shiukh, and they were part of the household economy.

The family residence patterns vary in form, but commonly we find nuclear family units and polygynous units. Attached to these basic forms we find other persons such as a father's widow, an unmarried sister, a widowed childless sister and/or various types of widows and their children. There are many patterns, and the particular pattern for the residence of a widow with children depends primarily upon two things: (*a*) whether she is from within the kin group and (*b*) whether or not she has a son. Let us take our previous case of the two widows again as an example. A man with two wives died. One wife was from a distant tribal section and had two daughters. The other wife was the deceased's cousin and she had a baby son and a daughter. The first wife lived with one of her husband's brothers but did not marry him. The second wife lived with her brother until the boy reached the age of twelve, and then the two wives and their children moved back to the husband's home, and the second wife became the head of the house until her son grew older.

A widowed father will live in his home with his youngest son and family. The father will still be head of the house and control the economy of the extended family as long as he is able. Occasionally one will find a residence which contains two brothers and their families. The brothers will be working off their father's debt and share the structure until the debt is paid.

The opposition between close agnatic collaterals which is a basic ingredient of organization among the Al Shiukh increases the desire of brothers to live in separate structures. Physical separation between close agnatic rivals is more easily accomplished in nomadic society (as is reported by Pherson, 1966:9) than among the Al Shiukh where immobile property and corporate ownership place limitations on mobility. The increase in tensions is often remarked upon by the inhabitants.

BRIDEWEALTH (*NAQD*)

Alliances through marriage are cemented by the transfer of a sizeable amount of money (often equivalent to one year's income) between the fathers of the couple. For example, in the case of a brideprice of 10,000 TL, the bride's father would give about 3,000 TL back to the bride and her husband for the establishment of their new home, thus the majority of the transaction is between the two fathers. We will see examples in the next pages of how a man who makes successful alliances, particularly those made with non-relative patrons outside the community, is able to gain local status by establishing more economic transactions through the arrangement of marriages. The patterns of these strategies and marriages will be examined. This is the major pattern of conversion from one political-economic system, that of the non-kin, to another, that of the kinship sphere.[2] The patterns of these strategies and marriages will be examined.

Permanent rights in the children of the marriages are acquired through the brideprice. Certain rights are also acquired by the patrilineage to the bride herself if she has children, and upon the death of her husband, she will remain within his kin group. A widow with children is either married in the levirate to one of her husband's brothers or to another member of the lineage. If she is from the lineage herself and has a son, she may refrain from marrying and eventually substitute for her husband or her son, or she may live with a co-wife who is in the substitution role just mentioned. If she has no children and is not of the lineage, she must return to her family and the brideprice must be returned or a sister given in her place. If she has no children and is of the lineage, her return will depend upon whether she has brought an inheritance with her. That is, if she has no brothers, and has inherited some land, she will probably be allowed to stay; if not she will go back to her home, or again her sister will be substituted with no additional brideprice.

The amounts of the brideprice are generally constant, according to the following social and economic distinctions, for the groups in this area. Less *naqd* is transferred between members of the same lineage, but there is a rise in the amount when marriage is contracted with a member of a related lineage, and again it is raised when it is with a person of another tribal section. For the Al Shiukh, the amount is approximately 5,000 TL for a lineage cousin, 9,000 TL for a cousin from a related lineage within the Al Shiukh agnatic segment, and 10,000 TL and up for marriage with a member of another tribal section. The variation in the latter amount relates to the landed status of the other tribal unit.

The fact that less money is necessary to insure the marriage of a lineage mate illustrates the strength of close ties which already exist in the lineage and underlies the bride's security in case her husband dies. The occurrence of exchange marriages within the lineage (*badala*) and the fact that a wife may become a substitute for her deceased husband if she is from within the lin-

---

[2]See Bohannan and Dalton (1962) for a discussion of economic spheres.

DESCENT, INHERITANCE AND MARRIAGE PATTERNS

eage further cement intra-lineage alliances and decrease the necessary amount of bridewealth. Furthermore, in the case in which marriage occurs between unrelated persons or between distantly related persons, the actual FBS who has the "right" of marriage to his first cousin and decides to claim it must be paid off. The money in this case goes to his father. This adds to the expenses of marriage outside the lineage, and although the price is fixed separately there is much quarrelling and bargaining over it.

Let us look at an example. A boy wanted to marry a girl from a related lineage. The girl's father was dead and her mother had only daughters. However, the deceased's second widow was from the lineage and had a son and was thus substituting for him as head of the family and the one who was to negotiate the brideprice. A mute FBS of the girl also decided he wanted to marry her, or more accurately, father wanted either the marriage or compensation and decided to press his claim. The girl's second mother wanted the first arrangement. The final tally worked out as follows. Fifteen hundred TL went to the FBS's father. Since the girl's father was dead, 1,000 TL went to her substitute father, her second mother; and 4,000 TL went to her only brother, her half brother. The latter's mother kept the money in trust for him. Twenty-five hundred TL went to the girl, and eventually went back into household belongings. The total of this amount was 9,000 TL. One can see from this breakdown that if many first cousins of the girl should demand their rights, the price would indeed increase greatly. In the case that a marriage is not desired with someone, particularly an outsider, this method of numerous claims is made to raise the price beyond possibility.

The dowry, or that given by the girl's family, is very small, unless we want to consider that they have given something by returning approximately one-third of the brideprice to the new bride and groom. If a girl's family is quite wealthy, however, we find that her father may give her something in addition, usually in the form of gold, but this is the exception rather than the rule among the Al Shiukh. The word *dota* (dowry) used elsewhere in the Middle East is not used in this region, and everything involved in the marriage transaction is referred to as the *naqd*. In previous days gold and animals were given as *naqd*, now it is strictly money, a few gold coins or jewelry and often a sewing machine.

A typical *naqd* for an actual FBD would be as follows:

Equivalent of twenty gold pieces given to the father of the bride equals about		3000 TL
Household		
3 beds of wool	@ 250 TL	750
3 quilts	@ 50 TL	150
5 pillows	@ 50 TL	250
4 sheets		
cupboard	@ 300 TL	300
1 good dress	@ 100 TL	100
5 average dresses	@ 50 TL	250
1 pair of shoes	@ 40 TL	40
1 jacket	@ 50 TL	50
4 big and small towels		
rugs for wall decoration	@ 200 TL	400
high bed	@ 300 TL	300
chest	@ 100 TL	100
belt	@ 250 TL	250
		5,940 TL

Eventually the father must also provide a house for his son and, if possible, some chairs, although these are recent additions to the desired acquisitions.

It is easy to see how the marriage wealth binds the son to his father from whom he must get the majority of this expense. If in addition to the above it is necessary to buy off additional cousins from the right of marrying the girl, it becomes an increasingly expensive and important contract. Since sons do not own land officially until their father dies, they will depend upon him almost entirely for this money in order to get married. We may add here that such a factor as the beauty of the girl may also enter into these computations slightly.

It is important to note the pattern of the relationship of brideprice, divorce and relationship of women to their affinal and consanguinal homes. We have noted that women are not totally absorbed into their affinal homes and not only retain protection in their consanguinal home, but also are punished through it. Yet we have no cases of divorces except in the case of a childless woman of another lineage, and we have high brideprices. The relative stability of marriage seems to be directly related to the importance of making alliances through marriage as well as the importance of the numerical expansion associated with the broadening and maintenance of power. Thus it is related to the total ecological position of the group not to the absolute factors of how much a woman is absorbed into her affinal home (Gluckman, 1950; Fallers, 1957). Nor does it relate totally to the different types of marriage (Leach, 1961:119).

Vengeance

Murder for revenge is greatly curtailed by national law enforcement, and blood money is used. Vengeance patterns are linked to status. Traditionally, if a shaykh killed a man of lower rank, the shaykh paid blood money. In the reverse case, the lower ranked person was killed and his family also paid money or labor or land. If he was an important shaykh, perhaps two or more men of the lower ranked family were killed. The vengeance unit involves agnates up to the fourth and fifth generations, but there has been a change in the pattern, and as it becomes more stratified, the genealogical depth seems to be regarded as less important. It was explained that the number of people killed in revenge also depended upon age. For each twenty-five years of the murdered man's age, one of the murderer's relatives had to be killed in revenge. Thus if an important shaykh of seventy years is killed, his relatives will kill three persons. Those upon whom the vengeance will be executed have to be sons or brothers of the killer. If the parties are from the same lineage or clan section, the killer and his family are exiled from the group. Another historical method used between tribal sections of comparatively equal strength, besides vengeance, was the giving of a girl to the parents of the murdered. No brideprice was received in this case.

The amount of blood money was 400 gold pieces for murder between equals and 200 gold pieces for dishonoring a girl (each gold piece is currently approximately 150 TL). Since the increased enforcement of national laws, the price of blood money has been reduced to 100 gold pieces.

One of the principle functions of the head shayk is negotiating blood money settlement between groups. It seems especially significant that a strong shaykh does the negotiating between the *agha* and lower classes. For here again such men serve as the middlemen between classes, and it seems significant that these religious kin groups operate in regions between the feudal urban and the tribal regions.

MARRIAGE PATTERNS ACCORDING TO RANK AND LANDHOLDINGS

Before analyzing the Al Shiukh marriages diachronically, let us consider their patterns in relation to those of other tribal sections in their region who differ in status, the amount of land they own and their degree of lineage localization. The first portion of Table 3 shows the patterns of marriage among four tribal sections that migrated from the same region in the Jazira (east Syria) and settled in the manner of core and fringe villages. In order, they represent: the Al Shiukh section which occupies a core village and has expanded its land ownings into the neighboring villages. Families cultivate 150 donums of land. They do not engage in agricultural labor. The secular Malik is a tribal section, some of whose land was acquired by the Al Shiukh and urban landlords. Part of the lineage migrated to Syria, and those that remained cultivate 25-50 donums per family head. They seldom engage in agricultural labor. The secular Naif section represents a former landowning lineage that became sharecroppers and workers after some of its lands were taken. The Faisal have a very small amount of land in a fringe village. Their original ancestor who settled there was given a small amount, for reasons which remain unclear. The members of this lineage must sharecrop in the village in order to supplement the proceeds from their small holdings. They average 10 donums per family head. They work primarily as sharecroppers on the lands of the landlord and landowning Al Shiukh and Malik groups in the fringe village. All these groups represent sedentarized societies; none is considered *hadarīya*, a term which is used by tribal groups for agriculturalists who work the land and are not from a tribal background.

In Table 3 the men's and women's marriages have been separated. The women's patterns vary more than do the men's. They range from 100 percent intra-tribal section marriages among the Al Shiukh, to 100 percent extra-tribal section marriages among the Faisal. This compares with a 72 percent intra-tribal section for the Al Shiukh men and 86 percent extra-tribal marriage pattern for Faisal men. In this comparison we may also notice that in the larger landowning groups, the men marry outside this unit more frequently than the women do; whereas in the landless groups, the women marry out as often or more often than the men do.

TABLE 3

MARRIAGES OF ARABIC-SPEAKING TRIBAL SECTIONS LIVING IN THE SAME REGION BUT DIFFERING IN STATUS, AMOUNT OF LAND OWNED AND LOCALIZATION OF KIN
(Computed Since Settlement: Four and One-half Generations)

Origin of Spouse	Men's Marriages: Different Tribal Sections								Women's Marriages: Different Tribal Sections								Men's and Women's Marriages: Different Tribal Sections							
	Sh %	No.	Ma %	No.	Na %	No.	Fa %	No.	Sh %	No.	Ma %	No.	Na %	No.	Fa %	No.	Sh %	No.	Ma %	No.	Na %	No.	Fa %	No.
ᶜAshīret (Tribe)	72	(115)	50	(15)	21	(3)	14	(2)	100	(11)	50	(8)	20	(2)	0	(0)	83	(226)	50	(24)	21	(5)	10	(2)
Non-ᶜAshīret	28	(46)	50	(16)	79	(11)	86	(12)	0	(0)	50	(8)	80	(8)	100	(6)	17	(46)	50	(24)	79	(19)	90	(18)
	100		100		100		100		100		100		100		100		100		100		100		100	
Marriages Within The ᶜAshīret (Tribe)																								
FBD/FBS	20	(31)	9	(3)	0	(0)	0	(0)	30	(34)	6	(1)	0	(0)	0	(0)	23	(62)	8	(4)	0	(0)	0	(0)
Lineage excluding FBD/FBS	28	(45)	16	(5)	14	(2)	7	(1)	40	(46)	25	(4)	20	(2)	0	(0)	33	(90)	19	(9)	17	(4)	5	(1)
Related lineage	24	(39)	25	(8)	7	(1)	7	(1)	30	(35)	19	(3)	0	(0)	0	(0)	27	(74)	23	(11)	4	(1)	5	(1)
	72		50		21		14		100		50		20		0		83		50		21		10	

Key to Tribal Sections (ᶜashīret):
a. Sh = Al Shiukh: Shaykh status, localized kin units averaging 100-150 donums per family head.
b. Ma = Malik: Medium to small landowners averaging 25-50 donums per family head. They are separated from the main core of the tribe.
c. Na = Naif: Former landowners, now scattered sharecroppers.
d. Fa = Faisal: A localized unit which averages 10 donums of land per family head and which also engages in sharecropping.

TABLE 4

PATTERNS OF VILLAGE ENDOGAMY AND EXOGAMY
(In Percents)

Location	Men				Women			
	Sh	Ma	Na	Fa	Sh	Ma	Na	Fa
Within same village	50	12	30	33	70	24	30	83
Out of 3 villages	23	88	70	67	0	76	70	17
Within 3 neighboring villages	27	00	00	00	30	00	00	00
Totals	100	100	100	100	100	100	100	100

Key to tribal sections same as Table 3.

From Table 3 and from material included in Table 4, the marriage patterns of each group can be summarized as follows:

a. Al Shiukh Shaykhs

The men of a successful lineage have a much wider range of mates than the women of that lineage. Upon settlement they arranged marriages with women of allied landholding lineages of agnatic groups equal to them and competitive to their adjacent successful agnatic rival. For example, the Muri are a successful group on the other side of their fringe villages. They have no marriages with the Muri,[3] but do marry with the group on the expanding agnatic core on the other side of the Muri. Then also both the Muri and the Al Shiukh have displaced weaker groups, and they do not marry with the particular group which they have displaced, but they marry with the groups which the other has displaced.

The next form of marriage for men is with women of their own and related lineages, that is, with Al Shiukh women. This form is most common since the women do not marry outside of the tribal section. The men may also marry women of lower ranking tribal sections. The latter are always polygynous marriages and are arranged with their sharecropping client lineage.

The women of the Al Shiukh lineages with whom we are concerned do not marry outside the tribe and, in our case, have not

---

[3] Represented by C(R) in diagram on p. 41.

DESCENT, INHERITANCE AND MARRIAGE PATTERNS   65

married outside the three lineages that live adjacently in these three villages. As we mentioned, the neutrality of the religious shaykhs explains in part why they do not give their women to form alliances with other tribes, but their ability to maintain this ideal is also due to their position of strength. A poorer section of the tribe that lives in another region is known to give its women to secular landowning tribes who have larger landholdings. When questioned about this, they initially reply that it is because that particular section of the Al Shiukh has more women than men. This of course is no problem for polygynous groups, and later they reluctantly added that the section is weak and because of its lack of land must disgrace itself in this manner.

Since residence is patrilocal, and the women do not marry out of the three lineages living in adjacent villages, the shaykh community is locally highly endogamous. The three villages were included on the table to show this.

b. Malik[4]

This tribal section consists of two lineages in a fringe village of the Al Shiukh in the Amik. They remained after their original core had been displaced in the struggle for land and relocated in Syria. While they live with members of an Al Shiukh segment, they do not marry with them, preferring to marry with the neighboring core that protected them (the Muri). They also marry with members of their section that have migrated to Syria as well as with another Malik core village in Syria to which those migrants attached themselves. Therefore, although there is a high percentage of marriages to relatives, they are highly exogamous territorially. In contrast to the landless groups, they follow the pattern of the landowning sections by marrying their own women to a high degree.

c and d. Naif and Faisal

These two tribal sections are primarily sharecropping groups with one difference between them. The Naif section is now completely landless, while the Faisal represent a lineage that owns a small piece of land in the fringe village in which the Malik and a section of the Al Shiukh reside.

Compared to the landowning groups, their marriages are tribally more exogamous; they marry by class with other sharecropping groups from other tribal sections. If they remain in

[4]Represented as X in villages FX on p. 41.

the same region, two such groups tend to carry on brother-sister exchanges; if this continues over a number of years, it results in patterns that include some cross-cousin marriages. The men also marry down if they become poor. Such a marriage would be with a woman from a shepherd's family.

The women of the sharecropping sections likewise primarily marry into their class and sometimes with their cousins. They attempt however to marry up into one of the landholding lineages, such as the Malik or Al Shiukh, in the area in which they engage in sharecropping. Due to this upward mobility through marriage for the women, their marriages reflect more exogamous marriages in terms of a tribal section, but are more localized in terms of residence than the men's marriages.

The difference between the Faisal and Naif patterns reflects the fact that the Faisal men have a piece of land which keeps them localized and allows them to get Faisal women from related landless lineages who sharecrop on other estates; they then give their own women to local landowning groups. The Naif, on the other hand, own no land now and move often, so that neither the men nor women stay in one region for a long period.

POLYGYNY AND THE DISPERSAL RATIO OF MARRIAGES

In the preceding section, the Al Shiukh were shown to engage in endogamous marriages to a much higher percentage than tribes of lower status and class. These figures are calculated in terms of absolute percentages and do not allow for the effect of polygyny on actual marriage choices. Since polygyny is more widely practiced among the Al Shiukh than by the surrounding tribes of lower status, a more accurate analysis of the actual frequency of certain marriages must be calculated with this factor in mind. To show this, the number of women married to the men in a particular tribal section in our sample is placed in the first section of Table 5. Then a ratio is derived: of the 122 married men of the Al Shiukh over four and a half generations, 31 have taken women in the form of FBD marriage, 31/122, or a ratio of 25; 45 have taken women from the lineage excluding FBD marriage, from which we derive a ratio of 37.[5] The absolute ratios of these figures are 19 percent and 28 percent respectively.

---

[5]This procedure, used also by Chelhod, was derived independently by the writer. This factor of polygyny makes Gilbert and Hammel's simulated model (1966) inadequate for this study, since they do not include it as a variable.

DESCENT, INHERITANCE AND MARRIAGE PATTERNS

TABLE 5

MARRIAGE DISPERSAL RATIO* BY TRIBAL SECTIONS
(Four and One-half Generations)

Tribal Section	Number						Ratio				Polygny Ratio
	Married Men	Wives	FBD	Lin	RL	OT	FBD	Lin	RL	OT	
Al Shiukh	122	161	31	45	39	46	25	37	32	38	134
Malik	27	32	3	3	8	16	11	18	30	60	129
Naif	14	14	0	2	1	11	0	14	7	79	0
Faisal	14	14	0	1	1	12	0	7	7	86	0

*Title suggested by Dr. Marshall Sahlins.
Key: Lin = Lineage
RL = Related lineage, same ^{c}ashiret
OT = Other tribal section

This ratio demonstrates the ability of a polygynous unit to simultaneously partake in different patterns to a higher degree than a group with no polygynous marriages.

From this table, it is evident that the Al Shiukh section combines exogamous and endogamous or close and distant marriages to a higher extent than the other less propertied groups do.

TABLE 6

MARRIAGE DISPERSAL RATIO BY LINEAGES OF THE AL SHIUKH
(Three and One-half Generations)

Lineage	Numbers						Ratio				Polygyny Ratio
	Married Men	Wives	FBD	Lin	RL	OT	FBD	Lin	RL	OT	
Salih	75	103	19	34	20	25	25	52	27	33	137
Hasan	8	10	0	0	7	3	0	0	87	37	124
Junayd	35	40	12	6	10	12	34	17	28	34	113

A further division of the Al Shiukh lineages into the three major lineages and then into sublineages shows the same principle operating (Table 6 and 7). Although this does not show the dynamic diachronic features which will be considered later, it is still possible to see that a lineage unit such as sublineage Mu in

TABLE 7

MARRIAGE DISPERSAL RATIO BY SUBLINEAGES OF THE AL SHIUKH
(Two and One-half Generations)

Lineage	Sub-lineage	Numbers						Ratio				Polygyny Ratio
		Married Men	Wives	FBD	Lin	RL	OT	FBD	Lin	RL	OT	
Salih	Ta	10	14	0	4	3	7	0	40	30	70	40
	As	19	20	2	14	1	7	11	70	5	37	23
	Ab	6	8	1	4	0	2	17	75	0	33	25
	N	3	3	2	0	1	0	66	0	33	0	0
	O	6	6	2	3	0	1	33	50	0	17	0
	Mu	22	38	12	9	7	10	55	41	32	47	175
	Y	0	0	0	0	0	0	0	0	0	0	0
Hasan	H	6	6	0	0	5	1	0	0	84	17	0
Junayd	Ah	7	7	2	1	3	1	29	14	43	14	0
	Mo	15	15	5	3	3	4	33	20	20	27	0
	Ar	15	18	5	3	3	7	33	20	20	47	20

Salih's lineage in Table 7 with a high instance of polygyny can engage in all forms of marriage simultaneously to a very high ratio. Others may be strong in the pattern of FBD marriage such as sublineage Mo in Shaykh Junayd's lineage but cannot compete in other forms with similar strength. This particular instance shows the overgeneralized nature of Cheldhod's argument in which he shows a direct correlation between polygyny and parallel cousin marriage. Here, on the contrary, the unit has engaged in FBD marriages at a ratio of 33, which is a high ratio, and yet there is only one plural marriage. Rather, the result was that the other forms were engaged in less often. Also Ta sublineage has a polygyny ratio of 40 but has no FBD marriages.

Tables 8 and 10 show the observed distribution of marriages within the patronymic group by sublineages and lineages. The relative size of each group has also been shown on the tables. The fact is obvious that larger groups can engage in more marriages than smaller groups and thus become economically engaged with more groups. The size figure in these cases has omitted children under the age of ten years (see Appendix I). Tables 9

DESCENT, INHERITANCE AND MARRIAGE PATTERNS 69

TABLE 8

OBSERVED FREQUENCY DISTRIBUTION OF MARRIAGES BY
SUBLINEAGE AND ORIGIN OF SPOUSE AMONG THE AL SHIUKH
(Two and One-half Generations)

Husband Lineage	Sublineage	Origin of Spouse											Brides Taken R_i
		Salih							Hasan	Junayd			
		Ta	Aw	Ab	N	O	Mu	Y	H	Ah	Mo	Ar	
Salih	Ta	0	2	0	0	2	0	0	1	0	1	1	7
	Aw	2	5	1	0	3	5	0	0	0	1	0	17
	Ab	0	0	0	1	1	2	0	0	0	0	0	4
	N	0	0	0	0	1	1	0	0	0	0	0	2
	O	1	0	1	1	0	2	0	0	0	0	0	5
	Mu	1	1	1	2	1	10	5	3	1	0	1	26
	Y	0	0	0	0	0	0	0	0	0	0	0	0
Hasan	H	0	0	0	0	0	5	0	0	0	0	0	5
Junayd	Ah	0	1	0	0	0	1	0	1	2	0	1	6
	Mo	0	1	1	0	1	0	0	0	0	7	1	11
	Ar	1	0	0	0	0	1	1	0	3	1	4	11
Brides Given	C_j	5	10	4	4	9	27	6	5	6	10	8	94
Sublineage Size	P_j	21	63	15	10	24	150	6	24	16	28	23	Total Size 380

and 11 indicate the marriage choices made by each group. It is important to consider choices and not people or marriages, since any marriage involves a decision by two households regarding the transfer of a brideprice; this also accounts for polygynous marriages. That is, a man married to four women will be counted four times himself, and the number of choices will be eight, not five persons or four marriages.

An attempt has been made to isolate the size factor and obtain marriage preference patterns. That is, if we can standardize size, we can still find certain preferences of groups for marrying with each other. The methodology employed in this process was used by Ayoub (1959) to find marriage preferences between differ-

TABLE 9

OBSERVED FREQUENCY DISTRIBUTION OF MARRIAGE CHOICES BY SUBLINEAGES AMONG THE AL SHIUKH
(Two and One-half Generations)

Husband Lineage	Sub-lineage	\multicolumn{7}{c	}{Salih}	Hasan	\multicolumn{3}{c	}{Junayd}	Total Choices
		Ta	Aw	Ab	N	O	Mu	Y	H	Ah	Mo	Ar	R_i
Salih	Ta	0	4	0	0	3	1	0	1	0	1	2	12
	Aw	4	10	1	0	3	6	0	0	1	2	0	27
	Ab	0	1	0	1	2	3	0	0	0	1	0	8
	N	0	0	1	0	2	3	0	0	0	0	0	6
	O	3	3	2	2	0	3	0	0	0	1	0	14
	Mu	1	6	3	3	3	20	5	8	2	0	2	53
	Y	0	0	0	0	0	5	0	0	0	0	1	6
Hasan	H	1	0	0	0	0	8	0	0	1	0	0	10
Junayd	Ah	0	1	0	0	0	2	0	1	4	0	4	12
	Mo	1	2	1	0	1	0	0	0	0	14	2	21
	Ar	2	0	0	0	0	2	1	0	4	2	8	19
Total Choices C_j		12	27	8	6	14	53	6	10	12	21	19	188

ent patronymic groups in a Druze village. Here it has been done between subsections of one patronymic group. An index, Nicholl's Index, was then used to demonstrate these preferences. The processes involved in this and the results obtained are included in Appendixes I through M.

If one turns to Appendix K in the back of the book, it is possible to compare Mu's and Mo's preference for marriage within their own sublineage once size is adjusted for. For Mu, preference for marriage within the sublineage is recorded as .0 on the Index and Mo's preference for marriage within the sublineage as .64. Mu's polygyny ratio is 175, compared to 0 for Mo. Again, then, by adjusting for size, we see how a unit such as the polygynous unit Mu, which has a large number of close marriages, also spreads them; while Mo's preference is highly concentrated.

The interpretation of the results will be more meaningful to

DESCENT, INHERITANCE AND MARRIAGE PATTERNS

TABLE 10

OBSERVED FREQUENCY DISTRIBUTION OF MARRIAGES BY LINEAGE AND ORIGIN OF SPOUSE AMONG THE AL SHIUKH
(Four and One-half Generations)

Husband Lineage	Origin of Spouse			Brides Taken R_i
	Shaykh Salih	Shaykh Hasan	Shaykh Junayd	
Shaykh Salih	54	6	7	67
Shaykh Hasan	8	0	0	8
Shaykh Junayd	9	2	18	29
Brides Given C_j	71	8	25	104
Lineage Size P_j	307	29	70	Total Size 406

TABLE 11

OBSERVED FREQUENCY DISTRIBUTION OF MARRIAGE CHOICES BY LINEAGE AMONG THE AL SHIUKH
(Four and One-half Generations)

Husband Lineage	Origin of Spouse			Total Choices R_i
	Shaykh Salih	Shaykh Hasan	Shaykh Junayd	
Shaykh Salih	108	14	16	138
Shaykh Hasan	14	0	2	16
Shaykh Junayd	16	2	36	54
Total Choices C_j	138	16	54	208

the reader after we discuss the dynamics and diachronic processes involved in alliance making. Also, since it is difficult to incorporate the change elements in these tests, they are considered secondary in importance to the analysis which follows in Chapter Four.

We may say, however, to better understand marriage patterns, we found it necessary to include the variable of polygyny, to separate male and female marriage patterns and to consider the affect of rank and landholdings upon the patterns. We have also attempted to understand the effect of unit size.

Through these processes, further understanding was derived about the patterns of endogamy and FBD marriage. In and of themselves, FBD marriages are not significant either, and they may mean different things. Their greatest significance occurs when they are combined with other forms of marriage by a successful group through the institution of polygyny. The fact that groups in the Middle East engage in endogamous and exogamous marriages has been pointed out before (Patai, 1965 and Cuisenier, 1962). However, the relation between the institution of polygyny and the ability of an achieving lineage to simultaneously engage in both practices has not been considered. Obviously such a group must be successful in outside alliances with other classes to have access to resources in order to provide sufficient funds for numerous brideprices. One may also note the direction of marriages according to the amount of brideprice. That is, in the index of preference for Mu, we see that a number of groups within the lineage have a positive preference for Mu brides, while Mu goes outside to a related lineage (H) to obtain a number of brides. As we may remember, the rate for brides from the related lineage is higher than for those inside. The direction of expansion was in the direction of the village in which H lived, and thus these alliances aided his expansion. Aw similarly has marriages with those of Junayd's lineage in the other fringe village.

Therefore we may conclude that a successful group does not encyst itself through FBD marriages. We may repeat that in connection with Chelhod's conclusion that parallel cousin marriage and polygyny are mutually dependent, it was independently found here that there is a relationship between polygyny, parallel counsin marriage and the general economic and power level. Yet within the more highly polygynous lineages there is no necessary direct relationship; for among the landowning Al Shiukh, one unit had a high ratio of FBD marriages and no plural marriages in its history. It is a weakened unit, and the strategy of encystment

DESCENT, INHERITANCE AND MARRIAGE PATTERNS

is one of protection only, not expansion. The significant point, then, is that the importance of FBD and "FBD" marriage is that it can be combined with the other forms to ensure protection of one's own resources through economic transactions (bridewealth) and extension to influence other's resources. This is achieved by successful lineages or segments such as Mu (Fig. 9), and therefore becomes the "ideal" pattern. In order to assure this pattern, strong segments will secure FBD or "FBD" as first wives if possible. It is obvious that marriage with a patrilateral parallel cousin is also preferred by a weaker and/or non-polygynous segment of the strong lineage, if this marriage aligns it with a strong segment.

Among landless groups, FBD marriages have quite a different function and are not as common as among landed groups. Since resource control is impossible and alliances are made primarily with patrons, FBD marriages are engaged in for the same reason as MBD marriages, that is, for convenience and being assured of finding a wife. But strategies which provide distant contact are often preferable to cousin marriages, and this would particularly be true if one could arrange a marriage of one's women with non-kin of a higher status.

Because the tests used in this chapter show the dynamic dimensions of marriage to a limited degree only, let us proceed with our analysis of political alliances, the struggle for land, brideprice transactions and marriage patterns over four generations of Al Shiukh settlement.

IV

MARRIAGE AND OTHER ALLIANCES BY THE AL SHIUKH IN THE STRUGGLE FOR THE CONTROL OF RESOURCES: A DIACHRONIC ANALYSIS

THE tests and tables of the previous chapter showed us the importance of considering stratification and polygyny in marriage patterns. In this chapter, we are interested in demonstrating the dynamic dimensions of marriage as they are used in alliance formation, and we have chosen to follow these processes among the Al Shiukh over four and one-half generations in order to understand the patterns more fully.

The basic reason for dividing the marriages into generations is the fact that the division of property, with the accompanying struggle for the control of resources and alliances which are cemented through the transfer of brideprice, are generational phenomena which are expressed through the arrangement of the next generation's marriages.

VARIANCE IN MARRIAGE PATTERNS OVER FIVE GENERATIONS

The following chart (Table 12) is introduced to show the difference in marriage patterns by generation in the lineage of Shaykh Salih, whose core village is Qariya in which the majority of the lineage now lives. The first generation is represented solely by Shaykh Salih's marriages. The fifth generation is incomplete, merely indicating the tendency of its patterns. The reasons for the differences will become clear in our discussion of the alliance patterns and their manifestations in each generation, but the chart allows us to observe immediately that there is a high degree of variation in FBD marriage when compared over several generations. For example, in generation three we

TABLE 12
TOTAL MARRIAGE PATTERNS CONSIDERED BY PERCENTAGES FOR FIVE GENERATION LEVELS IN SHAYKH SALIH'S LINEAGE*

Generation	FBD FBS % No.	FBSD FFBS % No.	FFBSD FFBSS % No.	FFBD FBSS % No.	FFBSSD FFFBSS % No.	FFFBSD FFBSSS % No.	FFFBSD FFFBSS % No.	RL % No.	OT % No.	Town % No.	NM % No.	Total % No.
1st								33 (1)	67 (2)			100 (3)
2nd		27 (4)						27 (4)	46 (7)			100 (15)
3rd	41 (24)	10 (6)	4 (2)	10 (6)				7 (4)	17 (10)	2 (1)	9 (5)	100 (58)
4th	17 (14)	8 (7)	35 (30)	7 (6)	1 (1)	1 (1)		14 (12)	10 (8)	6 (5)	1 (1)	100 (85)
5th		38 (5)	15 (2)		8 (1)	8 (1)	31 (4)					100 (13)

*Patterns are counted by choices of Shaykh Salih's lineage.
RL = Related lineages
OT = Other tribal sections
NM = Not married

find a high occurrence (41 percent) of actual FBD marriages,[1] whereas in the next generation, with even more such partners available, the figures fall to 17 percent while second cousin marriage has risen from 4 percent to 35 percent. From this chart, we may also notice that since the time of sedentarization, there has been a steady decrease in the number of marriages with other tribal sections. As in previous charts, these numbers are based on marriage choices.

Other studies have recently attempted to correlate time periods and marriage patterns among Middle Eastern populations and have divided their periods in a different manner. Cuisenier divided five generations into three periods which were characterized by differing external conditions and correlated them with the pattern of parallel cousin marriage among the Beudouin of North Africa. The conditions referred to the involvement of the Ansarine Bedouin in World War II, and he found the rate to be constant (1962). Chelhod most recently did a study in which he divided his sample into age groups which he terms generations. He likewise correlated the amount of parallel cousin marriage to external conditions, but noting the correlation of parallel cousin marriage and polygyny, he concludes that both are positively affected by periods of stability and negatively by periods of disruption (1965).[2]

The results of this study do not correspond to those of Cuisenier or Chelhod. It is found here that polygyny and parallel cousin marriage are directly correlated according to status, yet within a status level, there is no necessary direct relationship (see Table 7). Rather, it is the combination of several patterns which is significant to status. Second, since marriage arrangements were found to be a result of conditions in the previous generation in this study, it will be shown in the following pages that one of the highest periods of parallel cousin marriage followed a period of feuding over the division of lands during the sedentarization period. If Chelhod likewise correlated his marriage rates with the conditions of the previous generations, he would arrive at the same observation and the reverse of his conclusion.

---

[1]Gilbert and Hammel's mathematical formula which predicts the rate of FBD marriage expected by chance in a community cannot account for such a high percentage as 41 percent FBD marriages (1966).
[2]He fails to consider that his older age groups have had more time to accumulate plural wives.

PRINCIPLES OF DESCENT GROUP DISCORD CONTINUITY: MARRIAGES AND OTHER STRATEGIES

The struggle for succession and control of resources is reflected in the marriage patterns of the Al Shiukh. Our procedure of analysis includes a consideration of each generation from the original settlers to the present, and of the struggle for control of resources and the manner in which this struggle relates to the planning of their children's marriages.

It will be easier to follow the generational analysis if the following principles of factioning and alliance formation are outlined in advance, rather than summarized at the end. The following points can be observed in every generation.

1. The primary contest for leadership and the primary fission of the localized patronymic group which consists of three related lineages occurs between brothers of the strongest family of the strongest lineage. It is between full brothers if the family is not polygynous, between half brothers if it is. The eldest brother is always one of these contenders unless he dies at an early age, in which case the second eldest is brought up to take his place and unite the eldest brother's allies. The other contender is one of the younger brothers. The tendency toward primogeniture temporarily drives him out of the village to acquire vertical alliances with outside patrons and economic resources with which he returns to compete with his brother in alliance-making.

The new resources allow him to make alliances by giving more brideprices and also engaging in brideprices which are higher in amounts, that is, those with members of related lineages. He will acquire brides in this way for his children and occasionally for himself. The added resource also aids him in acquiring those few girls within the lineage who have inherited land. There is great competition within the lineage for these girls. Peters also found this competition in a Shi^{c}i village in Lebanon (1963) where women inherit and alienate land regularly, not just in the special case of having no male siblings as we found here. Also, in the village Peters describes, a woman's inheritance is equal to half that of her brothers.

In a herding economy, this conflict between brothers would be resolved more easily due to mobility and divisibility of pastoral property. With corporate land ownership, however, this departure accompanied by one's allies is not possible, and hence the contender returns to the village. The increase in tensions is obvious. The tendency toward primogeniture found among nomadic groups seems to become strengthened by sedentarization which requires more continuous and intense contact with urban society, as well as with other settled groups. In addition, however, the urban conditions and capitalization of land also provide alternative routes for a younger brother to rival his older brother's control. Emphasis upon demonstrated patrilineal descent also increases as sedentarization increases. The trend toward primogeniture is opposed by the ethic and ideal of equality of brothers laid down in Islamic inheritance regulations; but, as with women's inheritance, which is also stipulated in the Qur'an, the rules are manipulated.

If the family is polygynous, the half brothers ally together if one of them is a contender. If the half-brother unit holds no contender, it may split in its alliances, with the elder sons marrying their children to the elder contender's children, and the younger members marrying their children to the children of the younger rival (see Fig. 6). In addition to the nature of the division of alliances, the ages of the children seem to be more equal in this arrangement.

2. The second principle refers to the fact that alliances are cemented through the payment of brideprice from the father of the groom to the father of the bride. We have discussed earlier the fact that there is an inverse relationship between the amount of brideprice and social distance and also the fact that the "right" of the first cousin to marry his FBD or be paid off may be used to influence marriage decisions. In this respect, this "right" may raise the amount beyond the possible range of an alliance-seeker. It is also true that a person with additional resources is in a better position to pay off several demands or "rights" in order to acquire an important alliance.

3. A father will attempt to extend his influence as far as possible through the marriages of his children. If he is strong enough to have several wives, he will arrange the marriages of children from different wives in different directions of influence. He is therefore sowing the seeds of division between brothers or half-sibling units by this act.

Brother-sister exchanges are common in the case of marriages with relatives. However, they do not occur with outsiders since girls are not married outside the tribal section. If there are sets of half brothers, there is a definite attempt to make the exchange between full brothers and full sisters. The importance of the "unity of the womb" can be seen in this example.

Initially in the settling process of the Al Shiukh, we find that the exchanges of children within the three related lineages tended

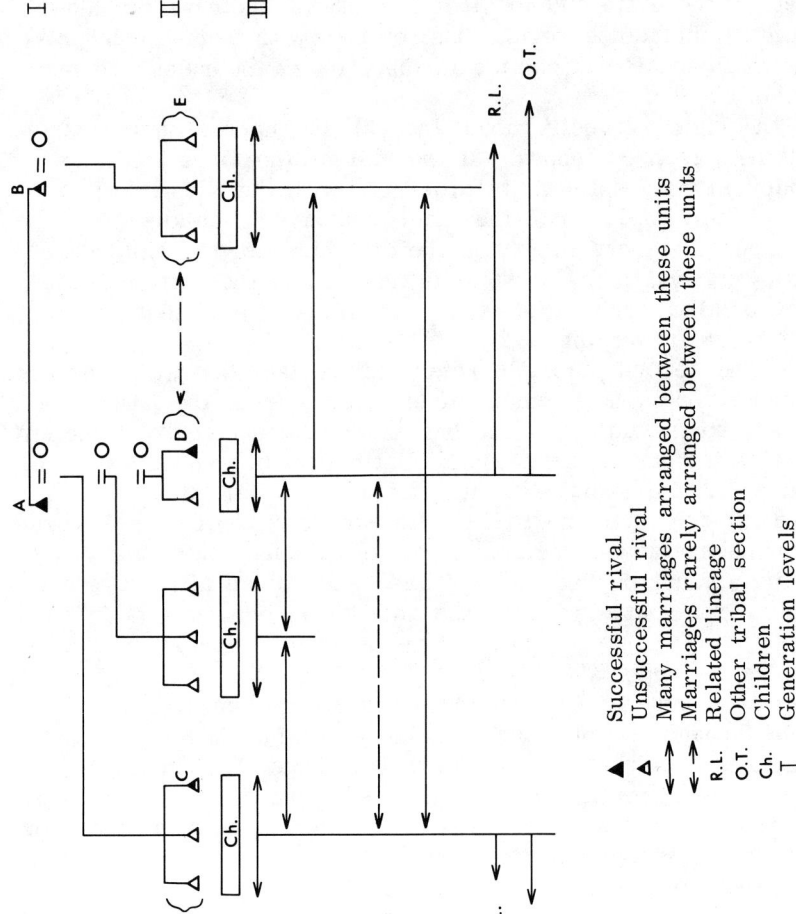

Fig. 6. Model of the ideal marriage patterns arranged between lineage competitors.

MARRIAGE AND OTHER ALLIANCES

Figure 6 represents the ideal plan of marriages between the children of brothers competing for leadership of a strong patrilineal unit. Note that there are few marriages between the competitors' children, i.e. between the children of A and B in the first generation or between C and D's children in the second generation. However, taking the sons of the successful competitor in generation one (A), we note that these sons (C and D) marry their children to their full brothers' children and compete to arrange marriages with the children of their half-brothers. C and D also compete in arranging marriages for their children with the children of the first cousins with whom they have few marriage ties themselves, that is, with unit E. The successful rival (D in this case) gains more of these marriage alliances than his competing brother C, and he procedes to unify the majority of the lineage.

to be with the mother's patriline. Since exchanges could not occur in cases where a mother was not a relative, and as biological descent became more important through the processes of sedentarization, capitalization of resources, and stratification, there was little concern about the mother's origin in planning marriages. If an exchange occurred with the mother's patrilineage, it was considered by the present group to be a coincidence.

4. The contending brothers, or units of half brothers in a polygynous family, arrange few if any marriages among their children.[3] That is, the idealized FBD marriage rarely occurs between units whose fathers were competitors for leadership of the descent group. Barth's observation that FBD marriage solidifies the lineage and overcomes cleavage between collateral branches (1954:171) is not common then to this case. The system under study stresses fa/so and bro/bro relations (see point 5 below), while Barth considers the bro/bro-so relation to be the most crucial. Transfer of money and resources is direct between the former relationships and only indirect in the latter relationship. The main schism of the descent group occurs between closest collaterals despite associated high rates of FBD marriages in the same generation. Point 5 shows why.

5. Although the contending brothers seldom marry their children together, they do compete to arrange marriages for their children *first* with the children of those brothers who do not oppose them. Therefore the preferred FBD marriage for alliances is clearly functional. The closest alliance one can have is with one brother against a rival brother.

We must then, when considering these marriages and relationship ideals between collaterals, cousins, etc., realize that they do not apply to all of the members of a classification, but to *some* of one's brothers, *some* cousins and *some* outsiders. The lack of strict descent group corporateness is illustrated by the following translated Arabic proverb, often used to describe very generally the Middle East segmentary process: "Me against my brother, me and my brother against my cousin, me and my brother and my cousin against the outsider." In reality it is more correct as follows: "Me against *some* of my brothers, me and *some* of my brothers against *some* of my cousins, me, *some* of my brothers and *some* of my cousins against *some* outsiders." Another proverb, "The enemy of my enemy is my friend," is closer to the actual segmentation.

---

[3]Over four and a half generations, marriages between children of competitors represent only .018 percent of all marriages.

6. The challenging brother, one of the younger ones, detaches himself from the established unit and tries to build his economic strength through external contacts, such as trading or serving as an urban landlord's steward on nearby lands. In the latter case, he may ally with a brother of the urban landowner with whom his own rival brother is aligned. Competition and reputation in healing quite naturally follow this struggle. The rival then uses his new economic resources to gain lands and form alliances through his increased ability to provide and secure numerous brideprices. He gains land usually through the practice of loaning credit to members of differing adjacent sections and is backed by his relations with the landlord and his new allies. He cannot gain additional portions of the original lineage patrimony, but may attempt to obtain land his competitor had added to the latter's share. In most cases however, differing rivals will try to gain land in different areas on the fringe of their core property. We therefore find that part of one sublineage has obtained property in Diya to the east of the village of Qariya; the contending unit has obtained land to the southwest in Koya. This difference is also attributed to the sphere of influence of the landlord with whom they align.

7. After the preference for marrying one's children to an allied brother's children, the next preference is with one's first patrilineal cousins' children, FFBSD. At this stage, an important pattern in descent group operation becomes clear, and explains why they can keep a corporate sense in spite of the processes of fissioning described above. The sons of the successful competitor in one generation are now the competitors in the next generation; and they compete with the sons of their father's rival brother, to ally that is, with members of the first agnatic cousin unit, with whom they have negligible generational marriage bonds themselves. These first agnatic-cousin units are not hostile then; but rather the stronger unit is split, and each segment tries to encourage weaker units to arrange their children's marriages with that segment. Within these general rules, there is some flexibility for personal choice since there are numerous brothers and cousins with whom one may align. However, throughout the system the desires of the children seldom carry much weight in the decision on marriage among the Al Shiukh. Propertyless groups have a wider choice, and their children have more say in the selection of their spouses.

8. As mentioned in the above section, the competition for control of the descent group passes to the sons of the successful brother, not the eldest sons of eldest sons. There is no fixed

rule, and so far in this lineage, it has varied from the youngest son of the youngest son, to the eldest son of the youngest son, to the youngest son of an eldest son. The age at death of the father does not seem to affect the outcome of who shall win the struggle. The eldest son uses the resources of his father, while the younger is forced to find new ones, and hence the main factor in the struggle is between the strength of these two origins of resources and the competitors' ability to use them.

9. If the actual blood members are not available, as they were not in the initial settling, a classificatory system is used. When Shaykh Salih and his real brother settled, they did not marry their children together, as they were rivals for the control of the land; but rather they married their children to children of "brothers" who were distant relatives unable to show their relationship, but who had allied with them. The marriages were considered as FBD marriages. The meaning of the terms "brother" and "FBD" marriage in their classificatory sense as the first and closest alliance attachment is clear. The system, therefore, smoothly incorporates distantly related and even unrelated persons.

The second circle of alliance attachment is with some of his second or "second" cousins, and the term "cousin" is used in the same classificatory sense of the meaning. The marriages are also called FBD marriages, but may be qualified by the addition of a patrilineage name.

10. In the case of a man who has no male heirs, he can never be a successful contender. One of his contending brothers will arrange marriages with his daughters, for these daughters carry one-half of his property with them.

11. The biological expansion at the center of the successful lineage due to the concentration of polygymous marriages is evident in Table 13. We note from the chart that of the 405 living descendants of the four original Al Shiukh settlers, over half, or 265, are descendants of the strongest settler, Salih. One hundred and forty-five, or over one-fourth, are descendants of Salih's son Muhammed, the strong rival in generation two, and 59 are descendants of Muhammad's son, Khalid, the leader of generation three. An average is presented for the number of descendants of the others by generation; however, it is given mainly for contrast, since those members closer to the core will have more descendants than those on the periphery of control.

Although the increase in the number of alliances and marriages results in an increase in the overall size of the unit, the external alliance with the landlord also allows the acquisition of new lands in which to place members of the expanding segments.

TABLE 13

NUMBER OF LIVING DESCENDENTS OF LEADERS OF
EACH GENERATION OF THE AL SHIUKH

Generation	Number of Males	Number of Living Descendents of the Most Successful Leader in the Generation*	Average Number of Descendents of Other Males in the Generation
1	4	265	47
2	13	145	23
3	39	59	9

*The number of living descendents today is 405. These constitute primarily generations 4 and 5.

Therefore, between members of the expanding ^{c}ashīret, the land distribution remains fairly equal (see Table 13). It was frequently mentioned that a large number of men was important in terms of political strength. This became particularly evident in the recounting of land disputes, many of which became violent. A man having many allies would be viewed by a landlord as a very desirable choice for an agent. Thus we may appreciate the degree of population pressure at the center of a dominant lineage, and we shall see below the manner in which that pressure is associated with expansion of the tribal segment from its center, thereby leapfrogging the periphery.

A DIACHRONIC EXAMINATION OF THE CASES

We shall now consider the total ecological situation of each generation, the conditions of land control and succession, and how these factors resulted in alliances which are observed in the arrangement of their children's marriages. It will be useful for the reader to refer to Figure 5 in this discussion.

First generation

Land and Succession

The first Al Shiukh settlers were two brothers, Shaykhs Salih and Omar. We have discussed how they obtained land by serving as mediators and trading middlemen, and how they themselves fought over the control of the region they had secured. Let us briefly review their settlement in the light of their alliances.

The two brothers camped in adjacent regions, now represented by the villages of Qariya and Diya. The elder one, Omar, died soon after the settlement and left his two sons in Diya. Neither son had male children and Omar's segment terminated. Salih then brought his "cousin" Hasan, of an opposing *fakhidh* of the Al Shiukh, and placed him in Diya and also brought his "brother" Junayd, of this same *fakhidh*, and placed him in another adjacent village, Koya. There were other tribal units occupying these villages, and we will remember that Salih accomplished this placement, which involved the acquisition of a share of the territory of those villages for Junayd and Hasan, through collaboration with the mountain Kurdish chieftain who promised to refrain from raiding these villages if a member of the Al Shiukh lived there. Certain shares of the grain were given to the mountain societies in exchange. Meanwhile Salih was renting a portion of land from a Turkman and employed a section of the Naif tribe to work the land.

The concept of a common pasture was kept by Shaykh Salih, who divided up the living area into three regions for his three wives and their children but, according to modern accounts, left no instructions for the division of the agricultural land.

Before Omar died, he and Salih were rivals for the control of the region, but Omar's early death gave Salih the control.

Alliances and Arrangement of Marriages

As the two brothers were rivals, they not only aligned their own marriages to different groups, but also their children's marriages. First let us consider their own marriages. They had both married into rival sections of the landowning Naif tribal section. Then they did not marry their children together in the traditional FBD marriages; rather Omar married his sons to women of an allied Naif section and his daughter to a member of the Al Shiukh faction that had lost in the struggle and retreated up the valley. Shaykh Salih married his sons to women of his allied Naif section, but in addition married his sons and daughters to children of the two related Al Shiukh members (Junayd and Hasan) whom he had brought into the region as allies. In addition to exchanging marriage partners between their children, Salih, Junayd and Hasan cemented their alliance by giving their daughters to each other as second wives.[4]

---

[4] Although Salih and Junayd were classified "brothers" ordinarily, because they were from the same political division, whenever the marriage of Junayd's daughter to Salih was discussed, members referred to them as cousins and the marriage as a FBD marriage.

MARRIAGE AND OTHER ALLIANCES 87

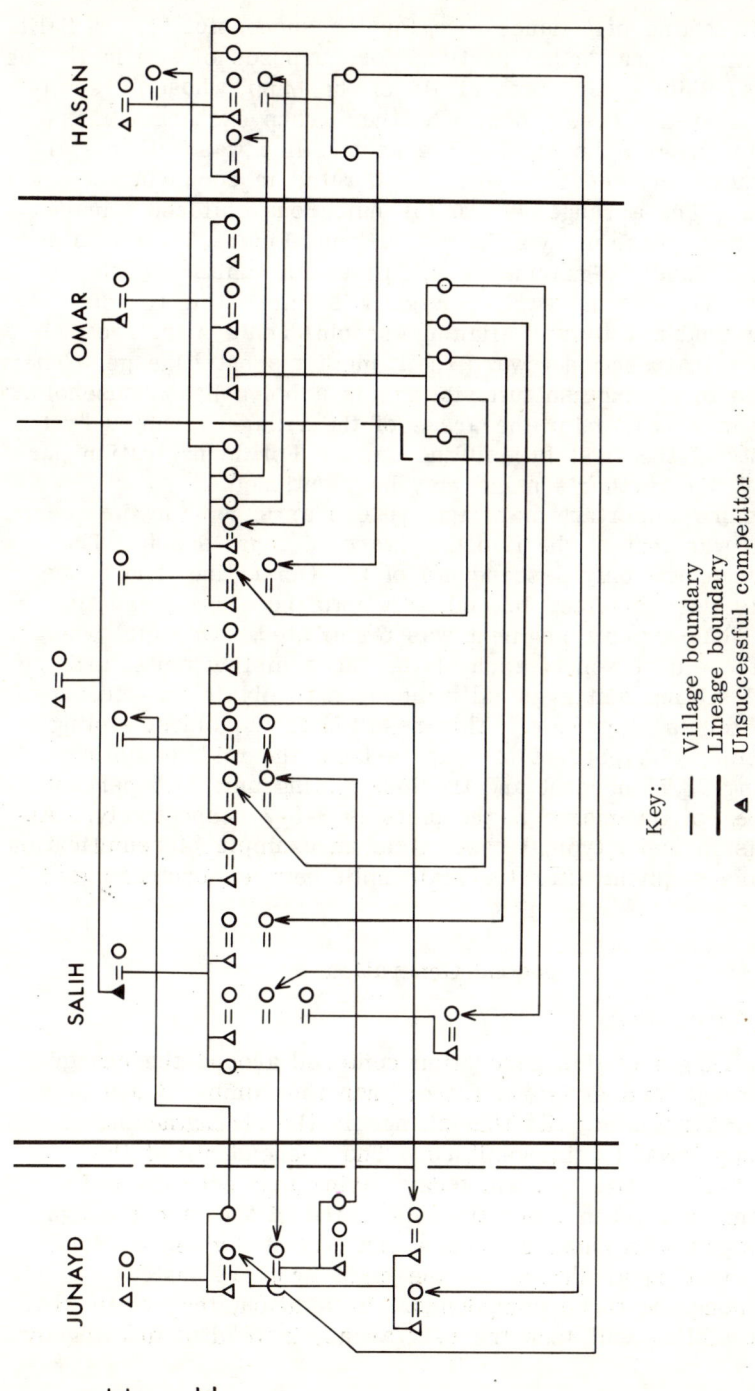

Fig. 7. Marriages between three Al Shiukh lineages first and second generations.

The first line of alliance then for the successful Shaykh Salih was with allied local tribal sections for purposes of settling. The Naif and Al Shiukh were both rivals of the Muri, whose core village was located between them. Neither group exchanged marriage partners with the Muri. The second line was with his allied "brother" and "cousin" who collaborated in occupying adjacent territories. The arrangement of his numerous children's marriages reflects these many alliances. From Figure 7 we also see that Salih aligned the marriages of full sibling units in different directions. During this early period, it is interesting to note that there is a tendency toward aligning the children's marriages within the tribal section toward their mother's patrilineage. There is no name to distinguish full siblings in a polygynous household, and there is no name for the areas of the village occupied by the descendants of the first full sibling units. For identification purposes only, the mother's name may be mentioned.

One more important marriage pattern arranged for the second generation was that of the five daughters of Omar's son. The daughters are the only descendants of the Omar line, and hence these girls were married immediately into the closest agnatic section. Thus Omar's segment was terminated. One girl was given to the eldest son of each of the three sibling units, and the eldest full sibling unit eventually managed to obtain the other two girls. In terms of property, this resulted in the oldest sibling unit obtaining 48.7 percent of Omar's land, the middle sibling unit gaining 28.73 percent and the last sibling unit 22.5 percent. The number of the males in the units is 3-3-2 respectively. Although this is not a typical case, it is an example of reunification of a lineage segment after the main split between brothers (see Fig. 7).

Second Generation

Land and Succession

The struggle of this generation centered around the change to agricultural land divisions rather than the combined use of a territory. Associated with this change is the strengthening of the tendency toward primogeniture. The descendants of the youngest sibling unit complain today saying that not only did the eldest compound claim more than its share of the land through the marriages with Omar's lineage, but that it divided up Salih's land into eight equal shares for the eight brothers instead of equally among the three compounds. In addition, they claim that the eldest sibling unit took the best areas, instead of drawing by lot for locations, and that sibling units one and two collaborated and gave only 5 percent of the movable property to their compound. This included furniture and animals. It was further claimed that the first two compounds split the sharecroppers 50-50, giving none to compound three.

This added control by the eldest brothers (particularly Taha) eventually drove the youngest son, Muhammed (a member of the youngest sibling unit), out of the village to seek new paths to success. He aligned himself with an urban landowner who had loaned money to weaker groups in the region during drought periods and had obtained their lands. The youngest son became the landowner's supervisor or *wakīl* for these lands, and thereby placed himself in a position in which he could also loan money. In addition he engaged in trade, serving as a middleman, and his prestige as a Shaykh, moderator of feuds and healer, rose accordingly. With these extra resources, he emerged in the region as a competitor to his eldest brother. He, like the urban landowner, acquired the titles to extra lands through lending money. This method is still the most commonly used method of gaining property in the region today. The land he gained was that land in Diya (originally Omar's land) which had passed to his brothers through marriage with the daughters of Omar's son. This youngest successful son, Muhammed, then placed two of his sons on this newly acquired land in Diya and his other two sons on his share of land in the core village, Qariya. He arranged their marriages with relatives in these respective regions. His four sons eventually married fifteen wives among them; the eldest son married five of the fifteen.

When the eldest brother, Taha, died, his younger full brother, Awad, consolidated Taha's allies to continue the rivalry with Muhammad. In order to strengthen himself and not being content with Taha's strength, which lay primarily with controlling the core lands, Awad also went out of the village and aligned with an urban landowner who was a rival to the urban landowner with whom Muhammad had aligned. In like manner, Awad obtained land in village three, that of Koya to the southeast, in which the Al Shiukh lineage of Junayd resided, and he moved some of his sons onto that land, leaving the others in Qariya, the core village.

Perhaps it is pertinent to recall the patterns of village occupancy here and the difference in these patterns among the villages. Qariya has remained a core village with a majority of the lineage living and expanding from there and, in particular, with the leader and his rival brother controlling the lineage property there. A contender may leave to gain backing; however, he returns to control the core village. The core village then never passes to the control of another tribal section. Both the strongest and the weakest members of the lineage live in the core village, while some sons of the strongest segment of the lineage branch into adjacent areas.

In villages like Koya or Diya which lie on the periphery of a strong expanding core village, we find, on the other hand, a pattern in which land changes hands and is accompanied by population shifts. The expansion by the dominant lineage segments is responsible first for placing related lineages there and then segments of the dominant lineage itself. The two related lineages are restricted in their expansion by the fact of their presence in the heterogeneous fringe village, and they expand very little. Thus they are affected by increasing population pressure and land fragmentation so that they may resort to agricultural labor themselves or to migration. Koya was already occupied by a tribal section and a member of the Al Shiukh, Junayd, was given a portion of the land in exchange for protection against the raids of the Kurdish chief. Many of the original tribal section were reduced to sharecroppers. Then, during the second generation, a member of the Al Shiukh, Awad, who was from a lineage which was of the core village Qariya, was able through urban alliances also to obtain land in Koya. His descendants strengthened their control at the expense of Junayd's lineage, and currently many members of Junayd's lineage must engage in sharecropping part-time. In this process, the urban landlord also obtained land in Koya. See Figure 5 and Tables 15 and 16 for the direction and amounts of land acquired during these expansions.

The case of the brother Awad realigning his full brother's allies through alliance with another landlord introduces a new element into the rural factioning. Urban landlords admitted to me that they took advantage of the factional nature of rural tribal groups to gain extra lands. In their relations with the non-tribal groups (the *ḥāḍariya*), such methods were neither as effective nor as necessary in acquiring lands. This division on the urban landlord level, which occurred in the several cases I noted, occurred among close collaterals in a manner similar to that described for the Al Shiukh.

Although this factioning involved in the urban extension of control has seldom been stressed in previous writing on Middle Eastern rural organization, it is viewed as fundamental to an understanding of both settled and nomadic organization of groups on the fringe of urban control. Hence we may say that within the Al Shiukh, rivalry has been increased not only through a

MARRIAGE AND OTHER ALLIANCES

transfer from pasture corporateness to control of agricultural land, which gives the eldest brother increased and longer lasting power, but also from the increased resources made available through urban patrons who are often rivals themselves and who purposefully foster rivalry in the rural regions. In this case the relationships involved the granting of individual land titles in an area of rainfall agriculture which led to the rise of large estates, the absentee landlord and his rural representative, the *wakīl*.

The availability of additional resources from the urban area meant that these resources were obtained first by an individual who then formed alliances with his additional wealth by providing numerous brideprices. Before sedentarization he had obtained additional resources through raiding with his existing allies. The diadic nature of the urban patron-client relationship therefore increased the individual's ability to gain resources.

In the following event we see an example of how urban patrons benefit from playing sides against each other, in this case with the Al Shiukh versus the Malik. During the Cadastral Survey conducted by the French in 1925, members of one tribal section in a fringe village mentioned to the surveyor that a piece of the other tribal section's land really belonged to the urban landlord, to which the other group responded in similar fashion, and the landlord received two new pieces of property. This clearly demonstrates the point mentioned earlier regarding the lack of corporate action in fringe villages allowing the government to stabilize plots which allowed further land acquisition by the urban landlord. In contrast, the core village continued to recombine fragmented plots, paid its taxes as a unit, and in general retained its flexible nature.

When the core village feels it is necessary to reorganize its shares, the members draw from a box for the position of their individual shares. They call the method, the *kura*, literally meaning "box." The divisions were made as follows: There are twenty-four original sections of land, which are considered to be of different quality. Each original section contains eight large divisions, which represent the inheritances of each of the sons of the original settler. The eight units are grouped so that plots of full brothers are adjacent to each other. The position of these eight sections within one of the twenty-four sections is determined by drawing numbers from a box. Then the descendants who have inherited land within each of these eight units draw again and again as they wind their way down the genealogical chart. The system is used when disagreements arise and

for the division of inheritance when a father dies. It is often
mentioned by the villagers that the *kura* is the ideal system as
no two plots are equal, but that in reality the strong members
of the lineage take the positions they want. There is also a
tendency to maintain the same plots year after year, and this
seems to be related to individual experimentation with fertilizers
and rotation of crops. The system of the *kura* is used here,
then, as an equalizer in terms of position and quality, rather
than quantity. The "box" is also used in principle for the order
of plowing, but again the stronger often get their way. Collective
ownership and management benefit the village as a whole, but individual usufruct provides situations that cause great strain
among agnates, and which constantly test the moderating ability
of the head shaykh. Attempts have also been made in fringe villages
to consolidate fragmented land by individuals exchanging plots,
but attempts are extremely difficult and bring much bigger problems than ever occur in the core village.

The increased urban contacts made alliance formation with
other tribes less important, and allowed an increase in internal
alliances and endogamous marriages. The ability to expand one's
lands began to include contracts with persons with whom marriages were not important; rather the contracts were vertical
and non-kinship in nature. This allowed a man to conserve what
he had and arrange marriages in order to exert influence over
close kin who shared resources with him. In Table 13 we see
this reflected in the marriages of generation three where only
24 percent are married to related lineages and other tribes,
versus 64 percent within the lineage. For the fathers' generation (generation two) 27 percent were with related lineages, 46
percent were with other tribal units and 27 percent within the
lineage. This represents a numerical increase of members within the lineage to marry, and we will remember that the marriages
of generation two with a related lineage were considered as FBD
marriages.

Alliances and Arrangement of Children's Marriages

The alliances of the two competing sibling units were formed
with the Al Shiukh clan lineages in separate adjacent villages.
Hence Muhammad had property in Diya and Awad had expanded
into Koya. They then married some of their children with the
related lineages in those villages. Marriages were also arranged
between children of full brothers within each sibling unit and to
unaffiliated half brothers of the other sibling unit that was in the

MARRIAGE AND OTHER ALLIANCES

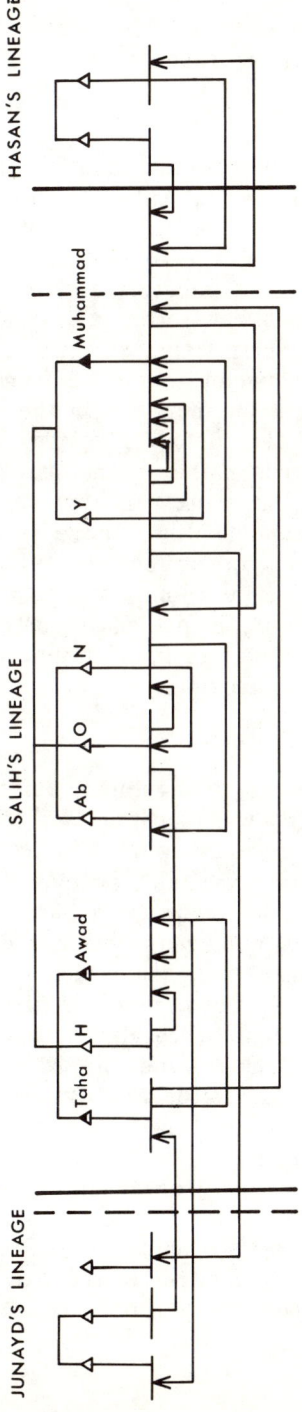

Fig. 8. Movement of brides in third generation arranged by chief lineage competitors of second generation.

Legend same as Figure 7.

middle position of this conflict and which resided in the core village, Qariya. This is a clear example of principles number four and five (see page 80). In Fig. 8, they are represented as Ab, O and N.

Third generation

The marriages of the third generation reflect the struggle between the two compounds of the strong Shaykh Salih lineage in the second generation. The fact that the first line of alliance in this struggle was within the full brothers sibling unit and with the unaffiliated members of the non-competing sibling unit, is evident in the new high (64 percent) rate of intra-lineage marriages compared to only 27 percent in generation two. Also the fact that of this number, 41 percent are between actual FBD and FBS. As mentioned, these figures represent an increase in the number of actual genealogical relatives and the factor of relying on cross-class alliances with urban landlords rather than local alliances with other tribal sections of similar rank. The marriages to related lineages went down in percentage since there is much intra-lineage marriage, but these marriages reflect the second line of alliance between the rivals, and hence remain important. The marriage to outside tribes, however, is not as important nor as frequent, and the relative number of this type of marriage has decreased from 46 percent to 17 percent.

Land and Succession

The youngest of the competitors, Muhammed, emerged as the strongest; and the next rivalry was between two of his sons, each of whom was living in a different region, Khalid in Qariya and Zeyd in Diya. The eldest son, Khalid, took over his father's position as *wakīl* and emerged as a strong contender. He eventually had five wives and with his numerous children dominated the marriage arrangements of the fourth generation in Qariya (see Fig. 9). The other contender, Zeyd, married his children with those of his ally, Hasan of Diya. The Hasan lineage never expanded numerically, and although it retained its land, could not expand nor help Zeyd's group expand either. Diya was a heterogeneous fringe village with two other tribal units in it, the Malik and Faisal, as well as land belonging to the urban landlord. The stabilization and permanent fragmentation of plots caused by the registration of land in the fringe villages eventually meant (1) a loss of ability by those segments of Salih's lineage in the fringe village to compete for control of the patrimony, and (2) made impossible any move back to the core village in order to control the majority of land.

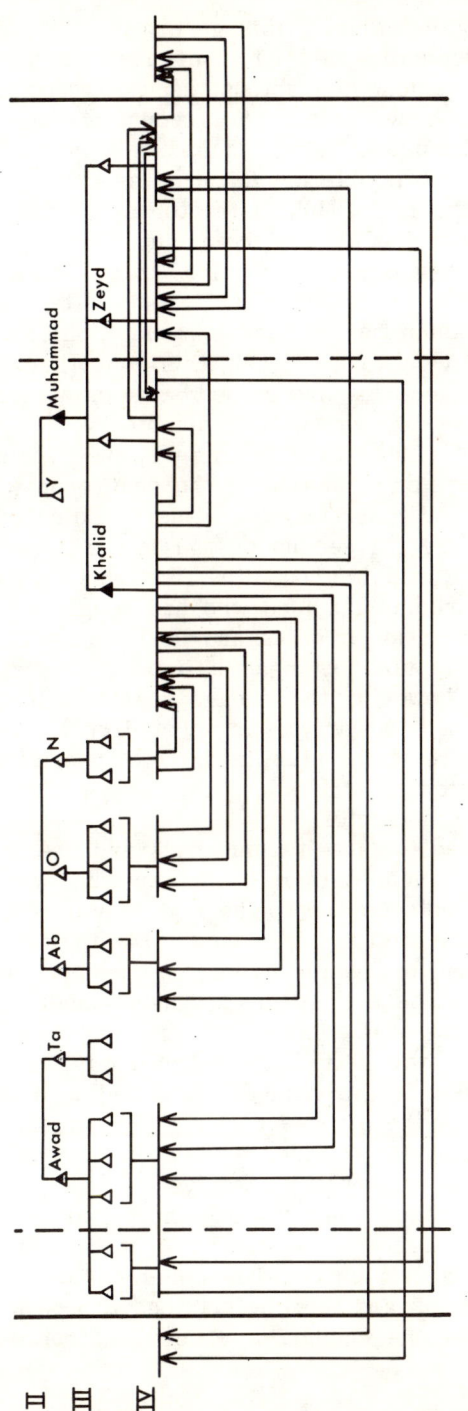

Fig. 9. Movement of brides in fourth generation arranged by chief lineage competitors of third generation.

Legend same as Figure 7.

The extra power gained during this generation through urban alliances by Khalid eventually went into increased economic control (through the management of tractors, seeds, etc.) rather than the actual occupation of new lands. The account of the core village's acquisition of the use of farm machinery clearly demonstrates its corporate and flexible organization as Qariya entered the machine age. In the late 1940's a tractor agent asked the Al Shiukh lineage whether he could rent their land. He would pay all the expenses, and they would be required to do nothing while receiving one-quarter of the profits after taxes. After much consultation and persuasion by the head Shaykh, Khalid, they agreed to rent it for five years. During this time they carefully studied the merchants' methods and gained substantial additional income. Besides the use of agricultural machinery, the new techniques included the use of chemical fertilizers, the elimination of the traditional fallow system, rotation of the cash crop (cotton) with wheat, and increased marketing facilities. Their corporate action allowed them to be the second village in the Amik Plain to adopt modern agricultural methods (the first was an estate owned by a wealthy Turkman landlord who had bought his own equipment). The stabilization of plots and the diverse lineage composition of the fringe villages made it impossible for them to enter into the project; however, the lineage segments in the fringe villages which are related to Qariya participated on a limited scale. The narrow width of the stabilized plots in a fringe village make the actual plowing of the long thin strips difficult and at times impossible for a tractor.

When Qariya decided to take its land back and use the methods which they had observed on their own, they could not obtain the same economic advantages due to the high rental cost of machinery and limited marketing privileges. But their fear of the tractor merchant and of the increasing of the economic power given to the head shaykh as the merchant's agent made the lineage decide to retain its local control.

As we mentioned, it was Shaykh Khalid who was instrumental in bringing mechanization to the village. He lived to be an old man, and he emerged as the strongest rival. This meant that the next struggle for control was to emerge between his sons, all of whom were living in the core village, Qariya.

Land acquisition ceased in generations three and four, yet the population kept increasing. The income, however, did not decrease for those groups which could mechanize, for they released their sharecroppers and thereby obtained that share. Those who could not use the machinery efficiently, that is, many

MARRIAGE AND OTHER ALLIANCES 97

in the fringe villages, suffered the population pressures and reduced incomes and some began to lose their status, to become employed on their own lands, or even on others' lands, or to migrate.

Generation four

The marriages of this generation reflect the struggle between Khalid and Zeyd as described above. Let us examine the figures. The population of the lineage is expanded biologically in Qariya, the region in which Khalid arranged the marriages between his children and his allies' children. Khalid's first line of alliance was with his brothers and his cousins that live in Qariya. Since there are more cousins than brothers, and since he has so many children, the marriages within the lineage reach a high percentage for second cousin marriages FFBSD at 35 percent. Zeyd, living in Diya, has his main alliance with the Hasan lineage, and hence the marriages for the whole lineage with the related lineages increase from 7 percent to 14 percent. This is due in part also to the fact that Khalid has picked up the alliance with Juneyd's lineage in Koya, the relationship once dominated by his father's rivals. (This is an example of principle 7 on page 81.)

The concentration of marriages in the two villages of Qariya and Diya from the children of Khalid and Zeyd is represented below:

TABLE 14

GENERATION FOUR COMPETITORS'
CHILDREN'S MARRIAGES BY VILLAGE

Village	Khalid's Children	Zeyd's Children
Qariya	13	1
Diya	2	5

The reunification of the main lineage in the alternate generation by a strong contender is clearly seen here in Khalid's ability to arrange marriages of his children with the grandchildren of his father's rival, that is, with Awad's children. We find then, that the successful rival in one generation is the one who can reunite the lineage successfully by arranging marriages with and hence allying the first cousin unit with whom he and his brothers share few common marriages in their generation.

The marriages to other tribes in generation four are down

from 17 percent in generation three to 10 percent. This is due to several factors, some of which we mentioned previously in discussing the growing localization of alliances as sedentarization continues. We may also mention that as the lineage becomes more stratified and larger, proportionately fewer men have plural marriages, usually only the sons of the rivals. In addition there are more relatives to choose from as the lineages expand. But in this generation, another factor that is important is that with the appearance of mechanized agriculture, the patron-client sharecropping relationship between the Al Shiukh *aghas* and Naif *fallaḥīn* has terminated, and the sharecroppers are physically out of the village as well as out of the economic and political activities of the village. Only the Al Shiukh core lineage of thirty families and three unrelated shepherd families remain in the core village of Qariya.*

Khalid's sons were the next to compete for control. Initially his eldest son, Hasan, held the strongest position, working with his aged father, Khalid, in the task of bringing machinery to the village. Actually Hasan died before his father and is an example of a man who died at the age of approximately fifty-six years and had never received his full share of inheritance. The second eldest son had worked closely with his eldest brother, and they had arranged the marriages of their children between them. He now holds the position of *mukhtār* or official head of the village of Qariya as well as of Diya and several of the absentee landlord villages.

But again we see the youngest son departing from the village scene, due to feelings of being slighted. He began trading animals and, through a rather complicated experience, he arranged a better deal with an outside merchant for renting tractors to the village. Thus he became the middleman for the merchant, was given seed to sell to the surrounding villages, and is now an important entrepreneur and powerful man in the core and fringe village region, earning eight times the average income of his lineagemates (see Village B, page 129). In fact he earns as much as many estate owners. Little of his income is made at their expense, however. Rather he rents and sharecrops lands from neighboring estates and villages. On some estates he pays all the expenses including the renting of a tractor and paying laborers and receives 80 percent of the profits. He also loans money to

---

*The figures also show more marriages to town women, but this is primarily accountable to one man who lives in the town and cannot be considered a trend. He is, in fact, not really considered part of the community since he has left his land. No city woman has ever lived in the village, although this particular man tried to bring one of his numerous wives to the village. The villagers would not allow it.

his kinsmen at a negligible rate. Contracts are sometimes made between lineagemates; those not involving interest are viewed most favorably (*rahanīya*), and sharecropping at 50% (*ortak*) is engaged in occasionally. Very recently, the head shaykh has rented some land from others in the lineage. This is considered an experiment, and some kinsmen view it with apprehension. (See page 123 for a discussion and definition of types of contracts.)

Neither the eldest nor the second eldest brother have arranged marriages for their children with those of this youngest brother. In the case of the eldest, the ages are too diverse, but the second eldest son has three wives and many children of the same age as his youngest brother's. Therefore the same basic patterns are persisting. The new young leader, however, has taken on some new attitudes in contrast to the second oldest son. The youngest son has only one wife and four children whom he hopes to educate. The second eldest has three wives and twenty-two children and is presently worrying very much about their future. Both brothers live in the same fashion as the rest of the villagers, although the *mukhtār* (second eldest) wears western clothes, while the young powerful shaykh dresses in the long white gown and black robe of the traditional shyakh. Both styles of dress are related to their work, the *mukhtār* must deal with the government officials, while the head shaykh is the healer, mediator and spiritual head of the region. When he enters the city, however, he wears the clothing of a well-off Turkish peasant, consisting of *sharwal* (baggy pants) and western coat with the *shabka* cap. It is primarily the texture of the clothing that shows he is not a poor rural person.

His ability not to depend upon numerous children for the purpose of alliances is due to the strength of his vertical contracts with the merchant. Still, he cannot buy the lineage property, and hence must maintain his traditional role in the village and live in a fashion similar to his lineage mates. His awareness of this fact has made him a successful leader, well-liked by the majority of the community. Through the structural elements of competition and corporateness which we have described, the lineage has been able to advance by following the leader who gets them the best advantage with stronger powers but is also able to check his control.

Land Size and Population Size

In Tables 15 and 16 we see that between patronymic groups, population growth and land size expand together in groups such as the Al Shiukh. For the Malik, population has increased and land size has remained the same or has decreased over time. Emigration helped the Malik group somewhat, however their man—land ratio is high (see Tables 15 and 16). A similar process occurs within the expanding Al Shiukh, for the core has increased through the Mu and Aw segments both in land size and population size, while a segment such as Mo has not expanded its property and has become crowded, forcing some of its members to do part time sharecropping. We should note that in Table 16B the Aw branch appears numerically small, but rights to produce are held by some Aw members who live in Qariya.

TABLE 15

LAND AMOUNTS AND CURRENT SIZE ACCORDING TO LINEAGE, SUBLINEAGE AND ᶜASHĪRET SECTION

Al Shiukh Lineage	Sublineage	Donums	Number of Families	Number of Persons
Salih	Ta	60	5	27
	Aw	1,700	10	63
	N	400	1	8
	O	550	3	16
	Ab	550	3	20
	M	2,000	19	146
Total		5,260	41	280
Hasan Total	H	350	4	18
Junayd	Ah	330	5	27
	Mo	330	11	54
	Ar	330	9	50
Total		980	25	131
Different ᶜAshīret Sections				
Al Shiukh		7,110	70	511
Malik		640	30	94
Faisal		160	13	50

TABLE 16

LAND AMOUNTS AND CURRENT SIZE OF GROUPS
IN CORE AND FRINGE VILLAGES

A. Fringe Village Diya

Ownership	Donums	People in Village
Hasan Al Shiukh	350	18
Salih Al Shiukh (Mu branch)	430	61
Malik	640	94
Faisal	160	50
Urban landlord	680	
Total	2260	223

B. Fringe Village Koya

Ownership	Donums	People in Village
Junayd Al Shiukh	1,000	133
Salih Al Skiukh (Aw branch)	1,000	23†
Urban landlord	1,000	
Total	3,000	156

C. Core Village Qariya

Ownership	Donums*	People in Village
Salih Al Shiukh	4,200	200

*Donums are rounded off
†Much of the land is held by members of the Aw branch in Qariya

Further comments

The lineage-core village societies of the plain are found to share more economic and political corporateness than kin groups of higher or lower rank and class, those with more land and those with less. In the villages under consideration in this study, corporate ownership, which was a survival from the previous nomadic institution of a joint territory, continued to protect the members against the uncertainties of plains agriculture after sedentarization and became a political defense mechanism against stronger forces in the area, both rural and urban. Initially they served as middlemen between the mountain and valley people in the struggle for control of and access to resources which follows sedentarization. Later, as we have seen, they maintained this intermediate position; this time via the new capitalization of land and the newly forming landed urban elite.

In a broad sense, we found the majority of a dominant and expanding lineage, those living in a core village, to be economically corporate. The patrimonial land is corporately owned, taxes are paid as a whole, roads are built and tractors rented jointly, fields are planted simultaneously and produce sold jointly. The fringe villages, due to their heterogeneous nature, were not able to resist government registration and stabilization of plots and the accompanying encroachment of the urban landlord on their lands. Thus, few of the advantages that came with collective tenure accrued to them. In the core villages, no member of the lineage can be denied a share of the patrimony, nor can anyone sell his share to an outsider or to anyone within the lineage.

If a member is in need of financial assistance, someone of the kin group lends him money or rents his land through one of several contracts, usually *rahanīya*. If he has borrowed from an outsider and cannot pay it back, members of the lineage immediately pay the debt back and arrange a loan with him. Anyone who behaves too recklessly is forced from the community and cannot retain his land rights. In the history of the kin group only two men have left for good: one because he murdered someone in the village and the other due to his immoral behavior.

Those members of the lineage segments which have expanded into adjacent communities and members of the related lineages also share in some of the benefits obtained by the dominating core. Such benefits include joint use of the tractor, loans advanced to aid early planting, and benefit in harvesting and selling. This economic political tie to the core village is basic to the lack of integration between various lineages in a fringe village.

The strength of the patronymic core to maintain its property in *mushā^{c}a* holdings officially is a sign of its corporate strength when compared to the weakness of the fringe village into which the urban landlord and the government cadastral survey gained an entry and some control. The stabilization of plots by the French cadastral survey in the mid-1920's was a result of, and further contributed to, the lack of coordination and efficiency in the fringe villages.

The fringe village continues its constant, time-consuming arguments over the endless measuring and remeasuring of plots. In this they even resort to hand and finger measurements. As a comparison of efficiency in the area of planting, in 1965 the core village measured and divided its land in three days and was able to plant one full month ahead of the neighboring fringe village. In the core village, the powerful head shaykh swiftly and carefully marked off the divisions with a rope while rock markers were put into place. The tractor drivers detest plowing in the fringe villages because the strips are so narrow that when they turn around they sometimes cross into a neighboring plot. This is particularly true at night when it is difficult to see the stone markers, and they inevitably become involved in the ensuing arguments. The segment of the expanding lineage which lives in a fringe village, therefore, can partake of only limited advantages through their relationship to the core of the lineage.

An interesting aspect of this study was the role of the shaykhs and particularly the head shaykh as economic middlemen and entrepreneurs. The first settler served as a successful mediator and ruled in a rural ecological shatter-zone in which both social and physical boundaries were changing. He was given the "first-fruits" or a sheep for his services. After sedentarization, the successful members of the lineage acted as agents of urban landowners, this time profiting by extra land acquisitions. This role has continued into the age of modern machinery where the head shaykh acts as a middleman and an entrepreneur in the renting of machinery to his kin and the selling of seeds to other groups in the region.

The situation in which the Al Shiukh adopted agricultural machinery gave us a good example of the corporate and non-corporate element of their organization as well as an example of the balancing of both tendencies for the good of the majority of the lineage members. An example of the control which the lineage has over the head shaykh is seen today in its insistence on renting tractors rather than borrowing money and buying them as a lineage. The government will lend them money if they subdivide their lands and register them, but it will not lend money on land that is registered in a dead man's name as theirs is. By refusing to register their plots they choose to spend extra money in order to check future control of their land by individuals.

It is interesting to note how the current amounts of individual land ownership in the core village tend to be equal after a century, despite the differential biological expansion created by polygyny. The primary levelling factor is the correlation of polygyny and resulting numerical increase of a strong and wealthy segment's population, to the power which allows such a strong segment to expand into neighboring communities and place members of the segment there. This method is no longer suitable, and very recently the extra resources gained by a strong segment are being used to send the male inheritors to school—thereby releasing their claim to the patrimonial lands. We may note the relative equality in income for a core village in Appendix F when compared (*a*) to a Turkman estate, and (b) to a village of ex-sharecroppers who were given 40 donums per family on reclaimed alluvial swamp lands some twenty years ago.

Other methods of levelling wealth which were discussed include distribution of the new resources through numerous brideprices, and the acquisition of more children which inevitably reduces the amount of individual land. Others may be cited: use of the *kura*; rotation of plots; the headman must provide for any guest (of which there are many) due to his function as mediator of feuds, and primary healer for the area; funds collected for any corporate project such as road-building, the building and support of the local school, and taxes to the government are scheduled. Any outside risk is assumed by the entrepreneur, either with the landlord, to keep him away from the patrimonial land, or to stand as security for loans during planting season for the community. Due to the limitations on his power imposed by the broad corporateness of the village and to the leeway in the contender's position to aid his lineage or himself primarily, there is a great deal of talk about a good shaykh or a bad shaykh. The holder of this position is closely watched by the lineage, but as in any power position, it can be used to aid oneself more or the community more, and gossip and attitudes of respect or lack of respect are constantly directed at it. Through these complementary structural elements of competition and corporateness, the lineage has been able to advance by following the leader who gets the best advantage, but it also checks his power.

In Appendixes G and H we have presented the items from which the village draws its income and those upon which it spends the income. In these charts we have separated the head shaykh's income and expenses due to the fact that he has become a successful farmer on lands in the neighboring region in addition to his participation in the village economy.

BEHAVIORAL PATTERNS IN LIGHT OF ALLIANCE FORMATIONS

Kinship Roles

The family relations that typify this region are similar to those that are found in other Middle Eastern family units. However, we might review them in the light of the preceding information on alliance formation, and also with reference to differences between groups of various socio-economic statuses. They are a reflection of the principal relation, that is between the two men who align and arrange their children's marriages together.

Fa-Son

There is a great deal of deference and respect shown by the son to his father and most of his father's brothers. This behavior becomes more intense after sedentarization due to the father's ability to retain management of his land until his death. With the noble groups, the sons are not obliged to aid their fathers in paying their bridewealth, but since tractors have been introduced into the village economy, the elder men who at least had the experience of managing sharecroppers complain that their sons have become lazy, thinking that all they must do is sit around waiting until the harvest comes in.

The young men must observe patterns of respect which are noticeably stricter than those of sharecropping groups. The young men are not allowed in the men's common room until the age of sixteen or seventeen, and they they sit at the place of least respect near the door so as to run errands. They seldom speak or join in the discussion, and their questions seem to be always directed through their fathers, or permission is asked of the father before asking a question. This permission is sometimes refused once the question is heard by the father.

The current youths of the Al Shiukh are being granted a share of their inheritance in order to go to school and learn a trade and are not expected to return to the village to live, but rather to acquire jobs in the city or as teachers.

In view of the nature of intra-lineage alliances, a son will not treat all his father's brothers equally. To the ones with whom his father is allied, and this often includes his father-in-law, he shows great respect and does many things for them as he would his father. To his father's competitor, he is certainly not disrespectful, but observes a polite and cool attitude, as does his father.

Since brothers often quarrel and split their alliances in different directions, and due to the fact that part of this division is created by their father's attempt to strengthen himself by aligning their marriages in various directions, the father will mediate and keep order among the sons as long as he lives and is capable. In his presence they do not fight. This restraining force certainly helps to keep the discord from much of its disruptiveness.

Among the sharecroppers, respectful relations may be shown initially in front of a stranger, but they break down much faster than among the landowners' sons. The fact that the father has no economic hold over his sons, and often the reverse may be true, contributes to the comparative freedom of the sharecropping youth. In contrast to landowning sons, sharecropping sons work for much of their brideprice, while the landlord provides a home. And since there is little property to pass on, there is little economic dependence of a son on his father beyond his adolescence. Finally, there is the basic factor of physical separation at a young age when most of the sons go off to find work where they can. This reduces the opportunities for relationships of filial piety.

Among the elite, of course, it is considered a disgrace if a man lets his sons work, and the extra earnings of a son would decrease the father's authority, which is not desired by any of the community for he might try to break his marriage bonds and upset pre-arranged alliances.

Brothers

The relationship among brothers, along with the father-son relationship, are two in particular that involve great sharing and mutual obligations. However, whereas the father-son relationship is always a united one among the Al Shiukh, due to the transfer of property, the brother-brother relationship is between supposed equals, and yet it has the potential for intense opposition or intense dependence and alliance. The relationship therefore can be characterized as varying from tense and competitive to cooperative or submissive, and yet to the outside these will both appear as united; for the tension is controlled and repressed waiting to erupt at another time, while the submission usually results in silence. Accompanying this tension is great suspicion. I found one brother often would tell me not to believe what another had told me. If there are half brothers, conflicts develop as with full brothers; but whereas both father and mother try to restrain the conflict in the case of full brothers, in this case separate mothers sometimes fan the conflict by their favoritism for their own sons.

Sister and Daughter

A young girl in the family receives secondary attention after her brothers, yet she is protected by her brothers and by her father in outside affairs, and by her mother within the family. In a core village such as Qariya, she knows that she will not be married into another tribe, and that she will never be further than walking distance from family in case she married into a related lineage outside the village, and that she will probably never have to do any manual labor other than household chores. For this privileged life, she must behave as one of the elite, with great respect and submissiveness to her male relatives in front of strangers. She must also show deference to older women. When she becomes twelve or thirteen, she must avoid boys of her age, since they are all her cousins and potential mates. If she is betrothed as most are, she is not allowed to speak to her fiancee until she is married. This may be five or seven or more years. During this period, she becomes extremely close to her brother, and a noticeable joking relationship develops. Previously, in their younger years, a son was allowed a freer hand in their quarrels, but as they become older they form a strong friendship together since they are excluded from close relations with their cousins of the opposite sex.

Sisters are close throughout their lives, particularly if they remain in the same village. As in the case of brothers, full sisters are much closer than half sisters since the alliance system may place half sisters in separate alliances. However, visiting patterns which allow a woman to return home and to visit her relatives may also create a line of communication between competitive groups which men cannot create.

The brother-sister role is also strengthened by the fact that brothers and sisters are often involved in exchange marriages to their cousins. For this reason, a brother keeps an eye on his sister's behavior, for his own marriage is involved in her behavior. And, as we have noted previously, it is his traditional right and duty to give his sister the ultimate punishment of death, as well as to try to obtain a divorce for her or to negotiate with his sister's husband to treat her favorably. In the case of a sibling exchange marriage, the consequences for one's sister of treating one's wife badly are obvious.

The father-daughter role is also that of protector and punisher. Men are given authority over women in most situations, and as with the increased power of fathers over sons and elder brothers over younger, men's authority over women also increases as importance is given to male descent. This authority however is shown particularly in front of other men and was relaxed somewhat in front of me. It is possible that a western male observing the Middle East would find a stronger sense of patriarchal behavior than a woman would. However, on all major matters men have the final word, and when a woman is recognized for her opinions, she has made a role shift, such as an unmarried widow who has control of property.

Collateral Relationships

Collateral relations reflect the alliances and splits made by marriages. Those between first cousins on the paternal side show a similar tense and cautious nature, alternating with extreme solidarity. Aligned cousins are obviously friendlier to each other and visit each other freely, while cousins of competing segments tend to meet regularly only in the *oda* of the shaykh. It appears to me that it is due to the tensions between such close collaterals who must reside and share property together, that we find the extreme use of circular means of communication. Such indirectness is expressed through stories, proverbs, and the use of a third person who is often the shaykh or an outsider. The third person usually does not actively engage in the conversation and is merely being used by two other parties. The head shaykh is commonly used as a third person and is conspicuously silent until he must make important decisions.

The *oda* then brings together the patrilineal collateral groups, tensions between which make it necessary to avoid direct relationships. In a village with different tribal sections in it, such as a fringe village, the *oda* operates to bring the sections together in the same fashion.

The term *khawāl* (mother's relatives) indicates an alliance when used between two tribes of equal status. Disturbances between these two groups are considered very serious and should be mediated quickly or tensions rise rapidly. If the marriage is between groups of different rank, the upper group pays little attention to *khawāl* relations for it is a relation of patron-client, an unbalanced relation. It is difficult to generalize in a ranked and stratified society regarding the relationship shown toward one's mother's relatives. Complimentary filiation does occur in marriages between close segments of the patrilineage, but is partially modified by common descent. Respect then is shown according to the system of alliance within the patrilineage. A boy's relation to his mother's brother would be different if that brother were also his father's first agnatic cousin than it would be if the mother's brother were a sharecropper or from a lesser lineage. There is a proverb in Arabic which is used to indicate complimentary filiation. "*Al-walid bītlak lakhālū*," or "The boy appears as his mother's brother."

Affinal Relations

As it is difficult to generalize on maternal collateral kin relationships we likewise cannot completely generalize on those of the affinal relationships either. In the case of son-in-law/ mother-in-law avoidance, it varies somewhat depending upon whether the mother-in-law is from the same patrilineage. If she is, the respect would become greater but not be an avoidance relationship. If his mother-in-law is not of his lineage, she will not live near him and he will probably seldom see her, so avoidance is natural. The same applies to his father-in-law, and again the relative status of the lineages of both members greatly determines their relationship.

The daughter-in-law relationship to her mother- and father-in-law is always one of great respect and submission. A daughter-in-law does not eat with her mother-in-law and must always obey her. This complete submission is symbolic of her role as the connector in an alliance. She is regarded as being capable of using the evil eye and is feared for this. She is talked about in terms of bringing good or bad luck to the family. The freedom of a woman to return to her home makes her an obvious object of suspicion to her new family, for she now has access to all their habits. The many jokes about mothers-in-law and daughters-in-law in the Middle East implies a tense situation. After she has had a son, this eases somewhat, for she is now a permanent member of the patrilineage into which she married. There are many cases however in which the two get along quite well, and in a polygynous household, a bride's mother-in-law may protect her from the remarks of the other wives. Again status is important, and an outside girl from a lower ranking tribal section may be treated a bit more roughly than a relative.

The husband-wife relationship involves a great deal of avoidance ritual. This begins at the time of their engagement in which they have a strict avoidance and non-speaking relationship which lasts until their marriage. After their marriage, they must also show near avoidance in public. This of course changes within the home.

In general, we may say that behavior corresponds to the political system in which brothers are either close allies or potential rivals. The tension implicit in such relationships is outwardly expressed by silence in implicit agreement, but formally glossed over rivalry is always present and is responsible for the lack of a "closed" mentality among the villagers. They are constantly prepared to look for opportunities to realign. Members of the leading segment look outside and inside the lineage, while weaker segments watch the dominant group in anticipation of alliances that will bring economic advantages. The core village, economically, politically, socially and psychologically, then, is closed in the sense that no one can get in, but is open in the sense that rivalry causes persons to make outside contacts. Any outsider put into this position quickly feels this combination of superficial tension-relieving indirect niceties and communal spirit, and simultaneously feels the impersonal desire by some to make an outside contact.

We may state again the necessity of interpreting attitudes and proverbs about relationships between relatives and to outsiders conditionally, since the dynamics of the system indicate that the ideal does not apply to all members of a classification.

V

CONCLUSION

THIS study focuses on a plain in southern Turkey on the Syrian border in which the processes of sedentarization in the nineteenth century and increased commercialization of land and production during the nineteenth and twentieth centuries have produced conditions of continuing stratification. Within this general situation, I am interested in examining different strategies of alliance formation and mobility in relation to land control. Using a diachronic analysis, the study inquires into the dynamics of kinship organization and the control of resources under changing conditions.

In order to understand the effect of aspects of sedentarization such as the granting of land titles, increased stratification and increased involvement with urban markets, it was necessary to consider the organization of the herders prior to settlement as well as the conditions of settlement. Thus, we compared the settlement of a highly ranked Turkman confederacy which had been engaged in long-range herding practices with the settlement of lesser ranked, short-range herders.

The result of the Confederacy's interaction with increased governmental pressures was a forced settlement and the development of an estate system whereby notables received and fought for large tracts of lands and engaged sharecroppers from lower ranking tribal groups. The lands of the notables became partially commercialized and agnatic kin groups were not corporate. Rather, political and marriage alliances tended to be bilateral and formed around a political division, both sides of which were controlled by a government-imposed family which had been of the rank of Pasha. The landless status and physical mobility of the sharecroppers on the Turkish estates are reflected in their marriages, the majority of which are with non-relatives and with persons outside their village of residence. Marriages aid in the communication of information regarding jobs and provide wide networks among the sharecroppers. Their relations with the notables are not accompanied by marriage relations and are strictly that of lord and sharecropper, patron and client. Throughout the area however, there is a general rule of hypergamy in which women marry on their level and up in rank and men on their level or down. Thus sharecroppers try to and occasionally succeed in marrying one of their women to a smaller landowning unit. This latter relationship often includes a sharecropping contract. They are not the same group that works on the large estates, but rather they live in the villages of medium and small owners described next.

The Al Shiukh are representatives of the short-range herding units. They have the rank of religious shaykhs and settled in a zone intermediate between the Turkmen estates in the plain and the mountain societies. Their organization was characterized by competing patronymic units which obtained smaller areas than the Turkmen notables, but whose success in expanding their lands is related to their corporate strategies and their alliances with patrons of a higher socio-economic class. These patrons were initially rural and later urban in origin, and in both cases the successful members of the patronymic groups served in the role of middlemen for the patrons. The settlement of these groups was not forced; they received their land titles primarily through the influence of their patrons.

The village patterns which emerged among these latter societies include patronymic core villages in which a dominant agnatic core holds its property corporately and expands at the expense of neighboring patronymic groups. The successfully expanding groups engage sharecroppers while some of these groups whose lands are reduced are eventually forced to subsist on smaller plots, engage in sharecropping, or migrate. Those villages located between the successful cores are called fringe villages, and the land holders are heterogeneous in composition since they include members of the expanding patronymic groups as well as members of the groups which have been expanded against. Part of the lands of the fringe villages may also have been obtained by one of the patrons with whom the expanding core had aligned. Until the recent introduction of machinery, both types of villages also contained numerous sharecropping families.

The corporateness exhibited by these successful agnatic segments is greater than that found either among those groups with more land or those with less, and their marriages are more endogamous. Alliances made with higher ranked groups are not accompanied by marriage in the case of the Al Shiukh. Rather the extra economic power gained from patrons is used for gaining control of additional lands and is converted into a position of leadership within the descent groups and local region by providing additional brideprices. The brideprices have been used to arrange the marriages of a man's children and occasionally to acquire additional wives for him. Marriages are primarily arranged within the patronymic unit, but also wives are obtained from allied patronymic units of equal rank. Some wives are also taken from groups from which a rival patroynmic group has obtained property, and the relatives of the bride would engage in sharecropping for the Al Shiukh. Marriages and alliances within the kin group are the highest at this intermediate level, with the most successful strategies combining different types of marriages through polygyny; thus the most successful are also the most polygymous. Recently, due to different factors, one of the most important being the fact that strategies of mobility now include sending young men to school and non-agricultural careers, a new pattern is emerging.

The collective ownership patterns of the Al Shiukh had their origin in the institution of nomadic joint territory. Collective landownership continues to protect the members against the uncertainies of crop return in an area of uneven harvests. It also functions as a defense mechanism against stronger forces, both urban and rural, and as a base for economic expansion and mobility. The increased pressures of governmental domination, the granting of patrimonial titles and the increase in local stratification creates an increase in general kin group corporateness and gives a new importance to demonstrated descent groups. Simultaneously, however, external relations increase the intensity of competition between patrilineal segments and members. I shall summarize these processes shortly; however I may add at this point that the study also analyzed the effect of the introduction of mechanized agricultural methods on the two general patterns, that of the estate and the core-fringe village pattern. The estates now are or are in the process of becoming farms which primarily employ seasonal workers and have forced the majority of sharecroppers to migrate to the cities or work as migrant laborers. Some were resettled by the government; most are impoverished. The corporate core village of the Al Shiukh also adopted machinery, released its sharecroppers and increased its total income. Its head shaykh has become a prominent entrepreneur and his income ranks with that of some prosperous estate owners, but his profit is not made at the expense of his lineagemates. The landowners of the fringe villages have benefited to a lesser degree due to a lack of corporate action and their inability to combine fragmented plots of land for efficient use of tractors. The plots in the fringe villages are stabilized while those in the core village are not.

After examining these different patterns of cultural adaptation, the focus of the study centers around a detailed analysis of the variables of succession, land control, strategies of alliance and marriage patterns of the Al Shiukh, over four generations, with comparative data drawn from groups representing different degrees of rank and landownership in the core and fringe villages. The relatively recent settlement of the Al Shiukh, combined with their pattern of joint patrimonial ownership and the highly endogamous nature of their marriage patterns, provide an opportunity for this kind of analysis within workable boundaries of space and time.

The result of the analysis is the development of an inductive model which demonstrates the patterns of opposition and alliance between patrilineal segments of the Al Shiukh as they are based on the struggle for land control and reflected in their arrangements of marriages and accompanying transfers of bridewealth. The model of integration demonstrates the method by which a strong propertied patrilineal core is maintained despite the fact that the main segmentary opposition occurs between the strongest brothers of the core. That is, in every generation two competitive brothers from the dominant core create the major external alliances, each with a different patron. Thus, within a generally corporate unit, closest agnatic units are socially separated, and relations of affiliation are distinguished from those of descent. Segmentary expansion occurred from the center of the dominant descentgroup and was associated with high rates of polygyny and increased population size. The segmentation also accompanied processes of land acquisition by expanding segments, and therefore we find the man-land ratio surprisingly similar for most segments of the Al Shiukh. Those soceites which could not expand or were expanded against witnessed a pressure of population growth on available lands and, as we mentioned, a portion were forced to migrate or engage in some form of labor. The same process accompanied the change from land expansion *per se* to economic control through neotechnic techniques. However, the head shaykh's economic advance has been proportionately greater.

In the process of alliance formation the majority of kin-based alliances of one generation are cemented through the arrangement of their children's marriages, while the primary bridewealth is transferred from the father of the groom to the father of the bride. Therefore, a synchronic analysis correlating marriages and conditions of the same period does not reveal the actual pattern of integration among the Al Shiukh. Also, some writers who analyzed marriage patterns over a time period, but correlated the marriage patterns with conditions of the same time period, actually have made a series of synchronic tests. Thus, as empirical verification of our model, the marriages in each generation are analyzed in relation to the variables of succession, land control and alliance formation of the proceeding generation.

We have said that the ideal or preferred marriage (and hence alliance) pattern of FBD marriage attains its greatest significance among these societies only when it is combined with other forms of marriage through the institution of polygyny. Obviously such a strategy establishes more economic bonds by providing and securing a greater number of brideprices. In this manner, it functions by allying and controlling a majority of a given segment's closest agnates and resources, while simultaneously extending alliances and economic transactions to more distant units. The system then is obviously a preferential marriage system influenced by rank and property, not a prescribed system as it has been treated by such writers as Murphy and Kasdan. In an earlier sentence, the words "allying and controlling majority" are important, for the data shows one important exception in the above pattern. The major rival aganatic units rarely arrange marriages between their children, and therefore have fewer direct economic ties and obligations. Thus collateral opposition occurs between closest agnates despite the accompanying high rates of FBD marriages. The latter occur because the contending brothers vie to arrange marriages for their children with the children of their other close agnates. There are many such agnates, particularly in polygynous families, and a further correlation shows us that the richest and strongest lineage segments have the highest rates of polygyny. The preference for FBD marriages is obvious. Who could be a closer ally than one brother who has allied with another brother against a third?

The descent group is not irrevocably split, however, and was found to maintain its continuity among the Al Shiukh in the following way. The process occurs in the next generation when two sons of the most successful competitor now become rivals. They likewise avoid alliances with each other, but their competition includes making alliances with the sons of their father's rival brother. This first cousin group is the unit with whom they themselves have negligible marriage connections. The most successful competitor obtains the majority of marriage arrangements, bridges the schism of his father's generation through the marriage of his children and thereby reunites the majority of the lineage. Thus, a three generational analysis is needed to show the major processes of fission and fusion.

The above processes operate in terms of classificatory relatives, and the presentation of various statistical tests made on actual marriage figures is secondary in importance without the model of integration. This was further demonstrated when we found among the Al Shiukh marriage patterns an increasing number of actual relative marriages through time as their localized population increased through biological expansion. The model still applies while its components represent different degrees of actual relationship. This point stresses the necessity of distinguishing between the principles of recruitment, descent and organization. Finally, behavioral attitudes toward relatives and outsiders, and the frequent use of indirect means of communication are analyzed in relation to those processes of integration.

Although different variations of these patterns are now emerging, particularly in relation to the relative increase in the wealth of the head shaykh, throughout our examination of the Al Shiukh under the conditions of continuing stratification, we have found the maintenance of a strong patrilineal nucleus based in property control. This nucleus contains the main segments of opposition and fusion and provides a simultaneous corporateness and flexibility or openness that is highly adaptive to changes and hence has a dynamic momentum, the understanding of which is necessary to this analysis of the relationship of culture and environment.

APPENDIX A

NINETEENTH CENTURY OTTOMAN TAPU DEFTER
DESCRIBING THE SETTLEMENT OF THE
REYHANLI CONFEDERATION

    The following two pages are copies of an Ottoman Tapu Defterli dated 1841 which represents the settling of the Reyhanli Confederation in the Amik. The third page discusses a petition from them that they be released from taxes that year.

PROPERTY CONTROL AND SOCIAL STRATEGIES

APPENDIX B

OTTOMAN LAND CLASSIFICATIONS

Mulk:

This is private land, and in the Ottoman era there was little of it. Primarily it consisted of buildings within a town or village. This classification was important under the first Arab conquests, for land was left in the hands of the inhabitants, and the lands were taxed one-tenth for Muslims, more for non-Muslims. Under the Ottomans the main categories of private property were *mawāt* (waste) land that a person cultivated and land assigned to non-Muslims.

Mīrī:

According to the Ottoman Land Laws (1858):

State land, the legal ownership of which is vested in the Treasury comprises arable, fields, meadows, summer and winter pasturing grounds, woodland and the like, the enjoyment of which is granted by the government.

Possession of such land was formerly acquired in cases of sale or being left vacant, by permission of or grant by feudatories (Sipahis) or Timars and Za'amats as lords of the soil, and later through the multazims and muhassils, (tax-farmers).

This system was abolished and possession of this kind of immovable property will henceforth be acquired by leave of the grant by the agent of the government appointed for that purpose. Those who acquire possession will receive a title-deed bearing the Imperial Cypher.

The sum paid in advance (Mu'ajjalah) for the right of possession which is paid to the proper official for the amount of the state, is called the tabu fee (Fisher, 1919:3).

State land was the most important legally; however with the weakening of the Ottoman Empire, it had the characteristics of private property. It was supposed to be registered but often was not.

Land from the state had certain restrictions on it. It could not be sold without the consent of the authorities, and the government tried to stop it from converting into *waqf*. In 1912, this was changed and a person could sell it. One could not turn it into *waqf* and if there were no relatives of a certain degree, the land became in *mahūl* and reverted back to the state if untilled for three years. Therefore a person only had a right of usage and right of transfer (except by will).

Matruke:

Land set aside for all inhabitants of a town or village, such as market, school, threshing floor, woods, pasture.

Mawāt:

Article six of the Land Code says, "*Mawāt* is land which is occupied by no one and has not been left for the use of the public. It is such as lies at such a distance from a village or town from which a loud human voice cannot make itself heard at the nearest point where there are inhabited places, that is a mile and a half or an hour's distance from such." As soon as *mawāt* land becomes cultivated it is *mīrī*, and the one who opens it can claim a deed to it.

Waqf:

Religious and family trusts in which it is said much of the land of the Ottoman Empire in 1858 was held. Originally in the family trusts, it could only go through direct lines, but the Ottomans allowed it to go to collaterals. Whole villages were often under *waqf* (Grannott, 1952:138). The Mamluk aristocracy owed their positions and survival to their posts as hereditary managers of important *waqf* foundations (*ibid.*). This type of land category has no divine character since the Qur'an does not command it explicitly according to the Hanifite School of Islamic Law which the Ottomans followed.

APPENDIX C

TYPES OF WORK CONTRACTS IN THE HATAY

Among the various types of contracts found in the area, the primary ones are the following:

Ortak or Sharik (sharecropping):

The owner provides the land and seeds, the worker provides the equipment and labor. Each pays half the expenses of seasonal labor. After the produce tax is taken, the laborer gets 50 percent of the crop. If the landowner provides the land only, he receives 20-30 percent after taxes.

Murāba^c:

The owner pays for all the expenses and the worker get 25 percent after taxes.

Icar:

The landowner leases the land for cash for a year or more. The renter pays all the expenses and gets the profits. On lands that rotate cotton and wheat, the usual term is two years. This form is replacing *ortak* as the area changes from wheat to the cashcrop cotton.

Rahanīya:

This system occurs between lineage mates. When one needs money he receives cash for loaning his land to another who pays the expenses and takes the profits. When the first man gets enough money, he repays the loan and takes his land back. Under this system, his land can never be lost to the other lineage mate due to inheritance rules.

ᶜAmala:

Wage laborers who are hired for various jobs for varying periods of time. Another form, ᶜAzab, involves the worker being hired for a year to do any job for whatever the landowner wants to pay.

In the pre-cotton period, the *ortak* or *murabe* system of sharecropping was the most common system, as we have mentioned. In addition, the fallow fields were used to pasture sheep and cattle, and the wheat sold as straw. Many of these herds belonged to the villagers themselves but they also were rented to mountain herders. In the summer, swampy lands near the lake were rented through *ortak* to villagers of the river regions who cultivated gardens for vegetables.

The *ortak* (50 percent) and *murāba*ᶜ relationships are being replaced by that of *icar* or *ortak* of the 20-30 percent variety wherever cotton and machinery are found today. The benefits for the leaser and leaseholder under *icar* depend on the amount of rainfall in a particular year. If there is a bad year, the leaseholder has lost the security he had as a sharecropper, and he suffers greatly. Also, as we have mentioned, machinery has replaced the majority of workers who previously shared in agricultural profits, and they work for reduced wages as migrant laborers. Most of the contracts made in the area today are verbal.

APPENDIX D

SETTLEMENT PATTERN OF SHARECROPPERS' MUD AND REED HOUSES ON A TURKMAN ESTATE: A FREEHAND SKETCH

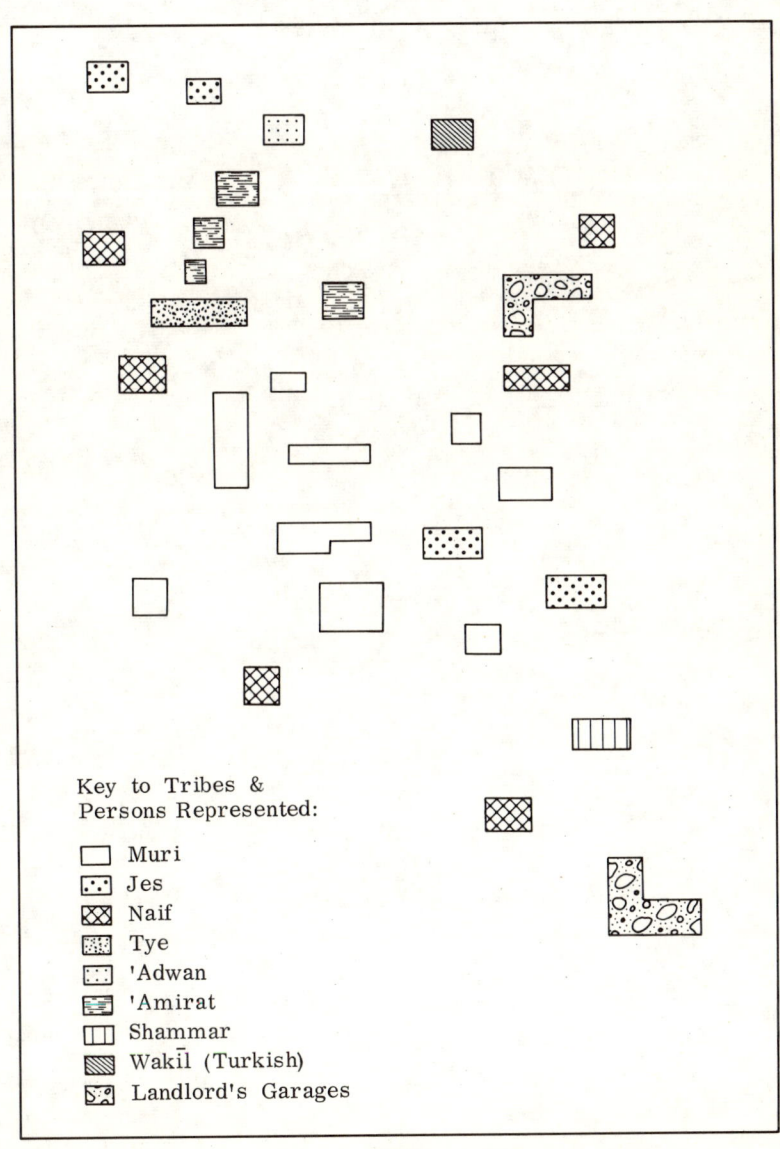

APPENDIX E

ANNUAL AGRICULTURAL WORK CYCLE

November—December: Half the fields are plowed for planting and planting is done if possible. Wheat and barley plowing is done by machinery.

January: A rainy month in which planting is completed. If the sun shines, the field are prepared for lentils and melons.

February: Old grape vines are cut, and the other half of the fields are plowed.

March: Fields are plowed as many times as possible.

April: Lands are measured and seed planted by machine for cotton, squash, watermelon and sesame. It is a very busy time due to the addition of newly born animals.

May: In early May the schedule is the same as April. It is the last opportunity to plant.

June and July: Fields are hoed. Barley, lentils and wheat are harvested.

August: A period of some rest. Grapes are cut. Wheat is cleaned. If there were water for irrigation, they would irrigate the cotton in summer.

September: Cotton is picked by seasonal laborers.

October: Same as September.

APPENDIX F

INCOME DISTRIBUTION OF THREE VILLAGES

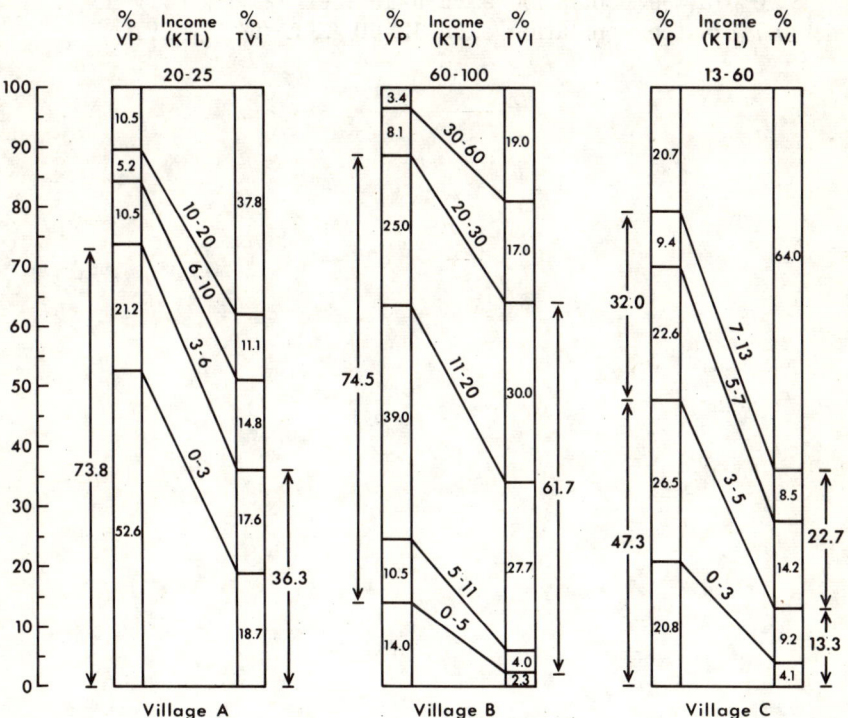

Symbols:

% VP = Percentage of village population
% TVI = Percentage of the total village incomes
KTL = Thousands of Turkish Lira

VILLAGE A: TURKMAN ESTATE (Without the landlord's income averaged in)
    73.8% of the population earn 6 KTL or less (36.3% TVI)

15.7% of the population earn 6-20 KTL (25.9% TVI)
10.5% of the population earn 20-25 KTL (37.8% TVI)

VILLAGE B: MUSHA^C CORE VILLAGE
14.0% of the population earn 5 KTL or less (2.3% TVI)
74.5% of the population earn 6-30 KTL (61.7% TVI)
11.5% of the population earn 30-125 KTL (37.0% TVI)

VILLAGE C: EX-SHARECROPPERS ON GOVERNMENT RE-CLAIMED LAND
47.3% of the population earn 5 KTL or less (13.3% TVI)
32.0% of the population earn 5-13 KTL (22.7% TVI)
20.7% of the population earn 13-60 KTL (64.0% TVI)

APPENDIX G

ANNUAL VILLAGE INCOME FOR CORE VILLAGE

Item	Percent Total Village Income	Average Per Household TL	Percent Households Receiving
Cotton	43.8	10,330	100.0
Wheat (sell)	26.1	6,160	100.0
Wheat (eat)	42.0	1,011	100.0
Animal products	2.6	1,210	50.0
Honey	.3	550	14.3
Fruit trees	2.2	670	78.6
Garden	.1	450	7.1
Trade (other than headman)	.3	1,225	10.7
Trade (headman)	2.1	14,500	.3
Loan (friend)	10.5	4,640	53.6
Loan (bank)	5.5	1,672	78.6
Shepherding	.9	3,000	7.1

Average income without head shaykh   17,768 TL
Average income with head shaykh   26,062 TL
Average for shepherd   2,700 TL

APPENDIX H

ANNUAL VILLAGE EXPENDITURES FOR CORE VILLAGE

Item of Expense	Percent of Total Village Expenditures	Average Per Participating Household (Turkish Lira)	Percent of Households Participating
New home	.9	1,333	10.7
Repairs house	3.0	715	64.2
Home furnishings	4.5	840	82.1
Clothes	6.9	1,069	100.0
Weddings (personal)	7.7	5,550	21.4
Weddings (village)	1.4	253	85.8
Other village ceremonies	.7	219	50.0
Doctors/medicine	4.3	717	92.8
School	5.2	1,127	71.4
Coffee, tea, sweets, tobacco	4.4	678	100.0
Travel to city	3.7	566	100.0
Guest room	.5	278	28.5
Food	15.0	2,292	100.0
Renting tractors	8.9	1,658	84.2
Hired workers and fertilizer	9.8	1,688	89.2
Animals care	7.3	1,741	64.2
Gardens	.3	160	25.0
Tax	.4	79	85.7
Interest (friend)	3.4	130	46.7
Interest (bank)	2.2	440	75.0
Loan repayment	8.1	3,136	39.2
Other	.9	466	32.1

Average expenditure without wedding: 14,114 TL
Average expenditure with wedding: 15,303 TL
Figures include head shaykh's expenditures.
Average expenditures excluding head shaykh: 13,380 TL

APPENDIX I

TESTS TO ISOLATE SIZE FACTOR IN MARRIAGE PREFERENCE PATTERNS WITHIN THE AL SHIUKH PATRONYMIC SECTION

In particular we shall use several tests employed by Millicent Ayoub in a Lebanese Druze village to show marriage choices between different patronymic groups while isolating the confounding effect of unit size[1] (1959). There are noticeable differences in our sample and results and those of Ayoub since our tests are concerned with preferences within subsections of one patronymic group and hers were between patronymic groups. Also differences occur in our processes of counting and the weighting of the raw scores. Ayoub used current marriage choices while we are including marriages over several generations. Her weighting includes all the living persons of the patronymic groups while we have omitted children under ten years of age in the villages currently. It was felt that to include them would be overrepresenting them since the population is increasing in each generation and their marriages will actually represent future patterns rather than existing and past ones. It should also be mentioned that the Druze are monogamous while we have seen that polygyny is important among the Al Shiukh.

In order to adjust for the effect of unit size, the actual frequency of marriages between units was observed and then compared to the frequency that had been adjusted for unit size. The latter frequency is called the "expected frequency" and was obtained by multiplying the total number of observed choices (R_i) of lineage i, by the proportion of the number of persons (P_j) in lineage j to the total population (P) of the units in the sample. The formula for deriving the expected frequency is:

$$E_{ij} = R_i \times \frac{(P_j)}{(P)} \text{ for } i, j = 1, 2, \ldots, N$$

where N is the respective number of lineages or sublineages.

[1] Although certain units show preference to marry with other units, the difference in the total number of marriages made by each group must be accounted for. For example, A may wish to marry with B, but if B's choices are used up, A must look elsewhere or to itself (Ayoub, 1959:270).

On Tables 8 and 10 we have shown the marriage distribution by the origin of the bride for the sublineages and lineages of the Al Shiukh. However, we shall be using marriage choices for our computation, not the number of marriages or the number of persons involved in the marriages. Choices are used since marriage as an alliance involves two decisions. Hence a man married to five women would be counted five times himself, and the number of choices is ten, not five marriages or six persons. The marriage choices are represented for the sublineages and lineages in Tables 9 and 11 respectively.

The expected and observed frequencies of choices were compared (Appendixes J and L), and the magnitude of differences represented on Nicholls' Index (1955:1). The formula for his Index is:

(Index) $H_{ij} = (O_{ij} - E_{ij})/R_i - E_{ij}$ when $O_{ij} > E_{ij}$

$H_{ij} = (O_{ij} - E_{ij})/E_{ij}$ when $O_{ij} < E_{ij}$

The range of his index is from -1.00 to 1.00, and it is calculated for every cell on the table (Ayoub, 1959:272).[2] The Indexes of preference for sublineage and lineage are presented in Appendixes K and M respectively.

---

[2] Quoting from Ayoub's article, the use of the Index can be further explained: "If the observed frequency for any cell on the diagonal is the same as the expected frequency, the index would be 0, and this would be interpreted as meaning that there is no endogamy or, in other words, that all the marriages of lineage i were made at random with respect to membership in i. If the observed were the same as the Row total, R_i, the index would be 1, indicating a state of perfect endogamy. If the observed total proved to be the same as the column total C_i, the index would be -1, implying an avoidance of lineage i and the state of perfect exogamy, which is to say again that all marriages made by lineage i were not made at random with respect to membership in i. When it is applied to cells off the diagonal, the index indicates in the same way the amount of preference which two lineages have for each other" (Ayoub, 1959:272).

APPENDIX J

OBSERVED MINUS EXPECTED FREQUENCY CHOICES BY SUBLINEAGE AMONG THE AL SHIUKH
(Two and One-half Generations)

Husband Lineage	Sub-Lineage	Origin of Spouse											
		Salih							Hasan	Junayd		
		Ta	Aw	Ab	N	O	Mu	Y	H	Ah	Mo	Ar
Salih	Ta	-.7	2.0	-.5	-.3	1.4	-3.7	-.2	.2	-.5	.2	1.3
	Aw	2.5	5.5	.1	.7	.3	4.5	-.4	-1.7	.1	1.0	.6
	Ab	-.7	-.3	-1.1	.8	1.5	.2	-.1	-.5	-.3	.4	-.5
	N	-.7	-.9	.8	-.2	1.6	1.4	-.1	-.4	-.3	-.4	-.4
	O	2.2	.7	1.4	1.4	-.9	-2.5	-.2	-.9	-.6	.0	-.2
	Mu	1.9	2.7	1.0	1.6	.3	.0	4.2	4.7	.2	.0	1.1
	Y	-.3	-1.0	-.2	-.2	-.4	4.3	-1.0	-4.0	-.3	-.4	.6
Hasan	H	.5	-1.6	-.4	-.3	-.6	4.1	-.2	-.7	.7	-.7	-.6
Junayd	Ah	-.7	-1.0	-.5	-.3	-.8	2.7	-.2	-.8	3.5	-.2	3.3
	Mo	-.2	-.5	.2	-.6	-.3	-8.3	-.3	-1.3	-.9	12.8	-.3
	Ar	1.0	-3.1	-2.5	-2.4	-1.2	5.5	.6	-1.2	3.2	.6	7.0

APPENDIX K

INDEX OF PREFERENCE OF SUBLINEAGE I FOR MARRIAGE WITH SUBLINEAGE J AMONG THE AL SHIUKH
(Two and One-half Generations)

Husband		Origin of Spouse										
Lineage	Sub-Lineage	Salih							Hasan	Junayd		
		Ta	Aw	Ab	N	O	Mu	Y	H	Ah	Mo	Ar
Salih	Ta	-1.00	.20	-1.00	-1.00	.20	-.79	-1.00	.02	-1.00	.02	.10
	Aw	.10	.25	-.05	-1.00	.01	.17	-1.00	-1.00	.01	.04	.02
	Ab	-1.00	-.23	-1.00	.10	.20	-.04	-1.00	-1.00	-1.00	.06	-1.00
	N	.11	-1.00	.08	-1.00	.28	.36	-1.00	-1.00	-1.00	-1.00	-1.00
	O	.17	.09	.11	.11	-1.00	-.45	-1.00	-1.00	-1.00	.00	-1.00
	Mu	-.65	-.31	.02	-.03	-.09	.00	.07	.09	-.04	-1.00	-1.00
	Y	.12	-1.00	-1.00	-1.00	-1.00	.45	-1.00	-1.00	.07	-1.00	-1.00
Hasan	H	.05	-1.00	-1.00	-1.00	-1.00	.67	-1.00	-1.00	.07	-1.00	-1.00
Junayd	Ah	-1.00	.49	-1.00	-1.00	-1.00	-.58	-1.00	.02	.30	-1.00	.29
	Mo	-.01	-.03	.01	-1.00	-.02	-1.00	-1.00	-1.00	-1.00	.64	-.01
	Ar	.06	-1.00	-1.00	-1.00	-1.00	-.73	.03	-1.00	.18	.03	.39

APPENDIX L

OBSERVED MINUS EXPECTED FREQUENCY DISTRIBUTION OF MARRIAGE CHOICES BY LINEAGE AMONG THE AL SHIUKH
(Four and One-half Generations)

Husband Lineage	Origin of Spouse		
	Shaykh Salih	Shaykh Hasan	Shaykh Junayd
Shaykh Salih	5.5	4.3	-6.4
Shaykh Hasan	12.8	-1.1	-.7
Shaykh Junayd	-24.5	-1.8	26.8

APPENDIX M

INDEX OF PREFERENCE OF LINEAGE I FOR MARRIAGE WITH LINEAGE J AMONG THE AL SHIUKH
(Four and One-half Generations)

Husband Lineage	Origin of Spouse		
	Shaykh Salih	Shaykh Hasan	Shaykh Junayd
Shaykh Salih	.16	.03	-.27
Shaykh Hasan	.86	-1.00	-.26
Shaykh Junayd	-.60	-.36	.60

BIBLIOGRAPHY

Anderson, J. N. D.
   1959 Islamic Law in the Modern World. New York.

Ashkenesi, T.
   1938 Tribes Semi-Nomades de la Palestine du Nord. Paris.

Aswad, B. C.
   1967 Key and Peripheral Roles of Noble Women in a Middle Eastern Plains Village. Anthropological Quarterly Vol. 40, No. 3:139-53.

Ayoub, M.
   1959 Parallel Cousin Marriage and Endogamy: A Study in Sociometry. Southwestern Journal of Anthropology Vol. 15, No. 3: 266-75.

Baer, G.
   1962 History of Land Ownership in Modern Egypt (1800-1950). Oxford.

Barth, F.
   1953 Principles of Social Organization in Southern Kurdistan. Universitee Etnografiske Museum Bulletin No. 7. Oslo.
   1954 Father's Brother's Daughters Marriages in Kurdistan. Southwestern Journal of Anthropology Vol. 10:164-71.
   1956 Ecologic Relations of Ethnic Groups in Swat, North Pakistan. American Anthropologist Vol. 58, No. 6:1079-90.
   1959*a* The Land Use Patterns of Migratory Tribes of South Persia. Norsk Geografisk Tiedeskrift Bind XVII:1-11.
   1959*b* Segmentary Opposition and the Theory of Games. Journal of the Royal Anthropological Institue 89, Pt. 1.
   1960*a* The System of Social Stratification in Swat, North Pakistan. *In*: Aspects of Caste in South India, Ceylon and North-West Pakistan, E. R. Leach, ed. Cambridge Papers in Social Anthropology No. 2. Cambridge.
   1960*b* Nomadism in the Mountain and Plateau Areas of Southwest Asia. The Problems of the Arid Zone. UNESCO. Pp. 431-351. Paris.
   1961 Nomads of South Persia. Oslo.
   1965 Political Leadership Among Swat Pathans. London School of Economics Monographs on Social Anthropology No. 19. London.
   1966 Models of Social Organization. Royal Anthropological Institute, Occasional Paper No. 23. London.

Bazantay, P.
    1935 Le penetration de l'enseignement dans le Sandjak autonome d'Alexandrette. Beyrouth.

Belin, A.
    1870 Du regime des fiefs militaires dans l'islamisme et principalement en Turquie. Journal Asiatique, Serie VI:187-302.

Bergheim, S.
    1895 Land Tenure in Palestine. Palestine Exploration Fund. Quarterly Statement. Pp. 191-95.

Berque, J.
    1959 Nomades et nomadisme en zone aride. Rev. Inte. Soc. Sci. Vol. 11, No. 4:481-98.

Berting, J. and H. Philipsen
    1960 Solidarity, Stratification and Sentiments. Bijdragen tot de Taal, Land en Volkenkunde Deel 116, 1e Aflevering, 54-80. The Hague.

Bilgili, M. F.
    1939 Kultur Hayati. Antakya. (Turkish)

Bohannon, P. and G. Dalton
    1962 "Introduction" In: Markets in Africa. Northwestern University Press. Evanston.

Boucheman, A.
    1934 Note sur la rivalite de deux tribes moutonnieres de Syrie, les Mawali et les Hadidin. Revue des etudes Islamiques Vol. 8:11-58.

Bowan, H. and H. A. R. Gibb
    1950 Islamic Society and the West Vol. I, Pt 1. Oxford.
    1957 Islamic Society and the West Vol. I, Pt 2. Oxford.

Burckhardt, J.
    1822 Travels in Syria and the Holy Land. London.

Chaoui, J.
    1928 Regime foncier au Syrie. Aix.

Chatila, K.
    1934 Le mariage chez les Musulmans au Syrie. Paris

Chelhod, J.
    1965 Le mariage avec le cousin parallele dans la systeme arabe. L'Homme Vol. 5, No. 3-4:113-73.

Chol, I. B.
    1934 The Yazidis, Past and Present. C. Zurayk, ed. Beirut. (Arabic)

Cohen, A.
    1965 Arab Border Villages in Israel: A Study of Continuity and Change in Social Organization. Manchester.

Cuinet, V.
    1890 La Turkey d'Asie geographie administrative. Four Vols. Paris.

Cuisenier, J.
   1962   Endogamie et exogamie dans le mariage arabe. L'Homme Vol. 3:80-105.

Cunnison, I.
   1966   Baggara Arabs. Oxford.

Daghestani, K.
   1932   Sociologique sur la famille musulmane contemporaine en Syrie. Paris.

de Planhol, X.
   1958   De la Plaine Pampaylienne aux Lacs Pisidiens. Paris.
   1959   Geography, Politics and Nomadism in Anatolia. International Social Science Bulletin 11:525-31.

de Reuck, A. and J. Knight, eds.
   1967   Caste and Race. Boston.

D'Ohsson, I.
   1924   Tableau general de l'empire Ottoman. 1788-1824. Two Vols. Paris.

Doukham, M.
   1939   Land Tenure in the Economic Organization of Palestine. S. Hamideh, ed. Pp. 73-109.

Eberhard, W.
   1950   A History of China. Translated into English by E. W. Dickes. University of California Press. Berkeley.
   1953*a* Types of Settlement in Southeast Turkey. Sociologues, N. F. 1:49-64.
   1953*b* Nomads and Farmers in Southeastern Turkey: Problems of Settlement. Oriens 6:32-49.

Elazari-Volcani, I.
   1930   The Fellah's Farm. The Jewish Agency for Palestine. Institute of Agriculture and Natural History Bulletin 10. Tel Aviv.

Empson, R.
   1928   The Cult of the Peacock Angel. London.

Evans-Pritchard, E. E.
   1949   The Sanusi of Cyrenaica. Oxford.

Fallers, L. A.
   1957   Some Determinants of Marriage Stability in Busoga: A Reformation of Gluckman's Hypothesis. Africa Vol. 27:106-21.

Farsoun, S. K.
   1970   Family Structure and Society in Modern Lebanon. *In:* Peoples and Cultures of the Middle East, L. Sweet, ed. Natural History Press. New York.

Fernea, R.
   1963   Irrigation and Social Organization Among El Shabana, A Group of Tribal Cultivators in S. Iraq. Comparative Studies in Society and History Vol. 6, No. 1.

Fisher, S.
    1919   Ottoman Land Laws. Oxford.

Flannery, K.
    1965   The Ecology of Early Food Production in Mesopotamia. Science Vol. 147, No. 3663:1247-56.

France, Government of
    1922   Rapport general sur les 1922 etudes foncieres effectues en Syrie et Liban, public pac les services foncieres du Haut Commissariat. Beyrouth.

Freedman, M.
    1958   Lineage Organization in Southeastern China. London School of Economics. Monographs on Social Anthropology No. 18. London.

Freeman, J. D.
    1961   Review of M. D. Sahlins, Social Stratification in Polynesia, 1958. Man LXI, No. 180.

Friedrich, P.
    1962   The External Relations of an Open Corporate Village. The Krober Anthropological Society Papers No. 27:27-45. Berkeley.

Frodin, J.
    1937   La morphologie de la Turquie sud-est. Geografiska Annaler Vol. XIX, No. 1-2:1-29.
    1944   Les formes de la vie pastorale en Turquie. Geografiska Annaler Vol. XXVI, No. 3-4:219-72.

Gellner, E.
    1963   Saints of the Atlas. *In:* Mediterranean Countrymen. J. Pitt-Rivers, ed. Mouton. The Hague. Pp. 145-58.
    1969   Saints of the Atlas. University of Chicago Press. Chicago.

Gilbert, J. and E. A. Hammel
    1966   Computer Simulation and Analysis of Problems in Kinship and Social Structure. American Anthropologist Vol. 68:71-93.

Gluckman, M.
    1950   Kinship and Marriage Among the Lozi of Northern Rhodesia and the Zulu of Natal, in African Systems of Kinship and Marriage A. R. Radcliffe-Brown and D. Forde, eds. Oxford University Press for the International African Institute. Pp. 166-206.

Goldberg, H.
    1967   FBD Marriage and Demography Among Tripolitanian Jews in Israel. Southwestern Journal of Anthropology Vol. 23, Summer:176-90.

Goody, J. (ed.)
    1958   The Developmental Cycle in Domestic Groups. Cambridge Papers in Social Anthropology No. 1. Cambridge.

Granott, A.
    1952   The Land System of Palestine. London.

BIBLIOGRAPHY

Granquist, H.
   1931   Marriage Conditions in a Palestinian Village. Societa Scientarium Fennica. Helsingforts. Vol. I, Vol. II, 1935.

Gray, R.
   1964   Introduction. *In:* The Family Estate in Africa, R. Gray and P. H. Gulliver, eds. Routledge and Kegan Paul. London.

Griswold, W.
   1966   Political Unrest and Rebellion in Anatolia, 1605-1609. Unpublished Ph.D. Dissertation. University of California at Los Angeles.

Guys, H.
   1853   Statistique du Pachalik d'Alep. Marseille.

Harik, I.
   1965   The Iqtā System in Lebanon: A Comparative Political View. Middle East Journal Vol. 19, No. 4:405-21.

Harper, G.
   1828   Village Administrations in the Roman Province of Syria. Princeton.

Hitti, P.
   1951   History of Syria, Including Lebanon and Palestine. New York.

Homans, G. C. and D. M. Schneider
   1955   Marriage, Authority and Final Causes. Chicago.

Horton, A.
   1962   A Syrian Village in its Changing Environment. Unpublished Ph.D. Dissertation. Harvard.

Hourani, A.
   1946   Syria and Lebanon. Oxford.
   1957   The Changing Face of the Fertile Crescent in the VIIIth Century. Studia Islamica No. VIII.

Ibn Ashur, I.
   1949   Metayage in Syria, Lebanon and Palestine. Al-Abhath I. (Arabic)

Inalcik, H.
   1955   Land Reform in Turkish History. Muslim World Vol. 45:221-28.

Jacquot, P.
   1929   L'Etat des Alaouites. Beyrout.
   1931   Antioche, Centre de Tourism. Beirut.

Joseph, I.
   1919   Devil Worship. Boston.

Kahhalah, O. R.
   1949   Mucjam Qabā'il al-Arab Vol. 1-3. Damascus. (Arabic)

Karpat, K.
   1960   Social Effects of Farm Mechanization in Turkish Villages. Social Research Vol. 27:83-104.

Kasden, L.
    1960   Isfiya: Social Structure Fission and Faction in a Druze Community. Unpublished Ph.D. Dissertation. University of Chicago.

Khair'allah, I.
    1941   The Law of Inheritance of Syria and Lebanon. Beirut.

Kirchoff, P.
    1955   The Principles of Clanship in Human Society. Davidson Journal of Anthropology Vol. 1.

Klat, P.
    1957   Mushaa' Holdings and Land Fragmentation in Syria. Middle East Economic Papers. Pp. 12-24. Beirut.
    1958   The Origins of Land Ownership in Syria. Middle East Economic Papers. Beirut.
    1961   Waqf or Mortmain Property in Lebanon. Middle East Economic Papers. Pp. 34-44. Beirut.

Kolars, J.
    1963   Tradition, Season and Change in a Turkish Village. Chicago.

Lammens, R. P.
    1906   Le massif du Djebel Sim'an et les Yezidis de Syrie. Melanges de l'Universite St. Joseph. Beyrouth.

Latron, A.
    1936   La vie rurale au Syrie et au Liban. Beyrouth.

Leach, E. R.
    1940   Social and Economic Organization of the Rowanduz Kurds. London School of Economics Monographs on Social Anthropology No. 3. London.
    1951   The Structural Implications of Matrilateral Cross-Cousin Marriage. Journal of the Royal Anthropological Institute 81.
    1954   Political Systems of Highland Burma. London.
    1961   Re-thinking Anthropology. London School of Economics Monographs on Social Anthropology No. 22. London.

Lescot, R.
    1938   Enquete sur les Yezidis de Syrie et du Djebel Sinjar. Berouth.

Levi-Strauss, C.
    1960   On Manipulated Sociological Models. Bijdragen tot de Taal, Land en Volkenkunde Deel 116, le Aflevering, pp. 45-54. The Hague.

Lewis, B.
    1951   The Ottoman Archives as a Source for the History of the Arab Lands. Journal of Royal Asiatic Society Pts. 3,4:139-55.
    1961   The Emergence of Modern Turkey. Oxford.

Lewis, N.
    1955   The Frontier of Settlement in Syria (1800-1950). International Affairs. Vol. 31, No. 1:48-60.

BIBLIOGRAPHY

Margoliouth, L. S.
    1965   Kādirīya. Shorter Encyclopedia of Islam. Pp. 202-05. New York.

Marx, E.
    1967   Bedouin of the Negev. Manchester University Press.

Meggitt, M. J.
    1965   Lineage System of the Mae Enga of New Guinea. New York.

Minorsky, V. F.
    1913   Kurds. Encyclopaedia of Islam. Pp. 1130-55. London.

Murphy, R. F. and L. Kasdan
    1959   The Structure of Parallel Cousin Marriage. American Anthropologist Vol. 61, No. 1:17-29.
    1967   Agnation and Endogamy: Some Further Considerations. Southwestern Journal of Anthropology Vol. 23, No. 1:1-14.

Musil, A.
    1928   Manners and Customs of Rwala Bedouins. New York.

Nicholls, W. L., II.
    1955   An Index for the Study of Homophily and Heterophily. Columbia University Bureau for Applied Social Research. Unpublished manuscript.

Nikitine, B.
    1956   Les Kurdes. Etudes Sociologique et Historique. Paris.

Orhonlu, G.
    1963   Osmanli Imparatorlugunda Aşiretleri Iskan Teşebbüsü. (1691-1696). Istanbul. (Turkish)

Palestine, Government of
    1945-1946   Survey of Social and Economic Conditions in Arab Villages. General Monthly Bulletin of Current Statistics. Jerusalem.

Patai, R.
    1949   Mush'a Tenure and Cooperation in Palestine. American Anthropologist Vol. 5, No. 3:436-45.
    1965   The Structure of Endogomous Unilineal Descent Groups. Southwestern Journal of Anthropology Vol. 21:325-50.

Pehrson, R.
    1966   The Social Organization of the Marri Baluch. Chicago.

Peters, E. L.
    1960   The Proliferation of Segments in the Lineage of the Bedouin of Cyrenaica. Journal of the Royal Anthropological Institute Vol. 90:29-53.
    1963   Aspects of Rank and Status among Muslims in a Lebanese Village. In: Mediterranean Countrymen, J. Pitt-Rivers, ed. Mouton. Paris.
    1965   Aspects of the Family Among the Bedouin of Cyrenaica. In: Comparative Family Systems, M. Nimkoff, ed. Boston.

Poliak, A.
    1939   Feudalism in Egypt, Syria, Palestine, and the Lebanon. 1250-1900. Royal Asiatic Society. London.

Post, G.
   1891   Essays on the Sects and Nationalities of Syria and Palestine. Palestine Exploration Fund, Essay 2.

Rafik, A.
   1930   Anadolu'da Türk Aşiretleri. Istanbul. (Turkish)

Rosenfeld, H.
   1958   Processes of Structural Change within the Arab Village Extended Family. American Anthropologist Vol. 60, No. 6, Pt. 1:1127-40.
   1968   The Contradictions between Property, Kinship and Power, as Reflected in the Marriage System of an Arab Village (Israel). *In:* Contributions to Mediterranean Sociology, J. G. Peristiany, ed. Mouton. The Hague.

Sahlins, M. D.
   1957   Differentiation by Adaptation in Polynesian Societies. Journal of the Polynesian Society Vol. 66:291-300.
   1961   The Segmentary Lineage: An Organization of Predatory Expansion. American Anthropologist Vol. 63:322-45.
   1965   On the Ideology and Composition of Descent Groups. Man Vol. 64, Art. 97.

Salim, S.
   1962   Marsh Dwellers of the Euphrates Delta. London School of Economics Monographs on Social Anthropology No. 23. London.

Sanjian, A.
   1957   The Sanjak of Alexandretta (Hatay): a Study in Franco-Turco-Syrian Relations. University Microfilms. Ann Arbor.

Schneider, D. M.
   1953   A Note on Bride Wealth and Stability of Marriage. Man Vol. 53, Art. 75.

Schorger, W. D.
   1969   The Evolution of Political Forms in a North Moroccan Village. Anthropological Quarterly Vol. 42:263-86.

Shim'oni, Y.
   1947   The Arabs of Palestine Translated by Leo Neubart. Human Relations Areas Files. New Haven.

Sinha, S.
   1967   Caste in India: Its Essential Pattern of Socio-Cultural Integration. *In:* Caste and Race. A. de Reuch and J. Knight, eds. Pp. 92-105. Boston.

Sterling, P.
   1957   Land, Marriage and the Law in Turkish Villages. International Social Science Bulletin Vol. IX:21-33.
   1965   Turkish Village. London.

Sweet, L.
   1960   Tell Toqaan: A Syrian Village. Anthropological Papers, Museum of Anthropology, University of Michigan No. 4. Ann Arbor.

1965 Camel Pastoralism in North Arabia and the Minimal Camping Unit. *In*: Man, Culture and Animals. AAAS No. 78. Leeds and Vayda, eds. Pp. 129-52. Washington, D.C.

Sykes, M.
1915 The Caliph's Last Heritage. London.

Tchalenko, G.
1953 Villages Antiques de la Syria du Nord Vols. I and II; Vol. III. Paris.

Titiev, M.
1943 Influence of Common Residence on Unilineal Classification of Kin. American Anthropologist Vol. 45.

Thoumin, R.
1936 Geographie humaine de la Syrie centrale. Paris.

Turkey, Government of
1841 Tapu ve Kadastro Umum Müdülügü Arşivi. Tapu Defterleri Mufassal Liwa Aleppo Vol. 36. (Inserted section in 15th Century Defter of the Liwa of Aleppo.) Ankara. (Turkish)
1948 Devlet Istatistik Enstitüsü. Köyler Islatistigi. Köy Sayuni. Hulâsu Sonuçlari. (Village Census Summary Results) Publ. No. 340. Ankara. (Turkish)
1961 Bayindirlik Bakanligi, Devlet Su Işleri Genel Müdürlügü. Amik Ovasi Zirai Ekonomi Raporu (Planlama Kademesinde). Zirai Ekonomi Etud Raporlari No. 17, B-1. Ankara. (Turkish)
n.d. Köy Işleri Bakanligi Yayinlari. Köy Envanter Etüdlerine Göre: Hatay. Ankara. (Turkish)

Türkman, F. A.
1937 Hatay Cografyasi ve Edebiyat. Cümhüriyet Matbaasi. Istanbul. (Turkish)

Turner, V. W.
1957 Schism and Continuity in an African Society. Manchester University Press.

Tute, R. C.
1927 The Ottoman Land Laws, with a Commentary on the Ottoman Land Code of 7th Ramadan 1274. Jerusalem.

Üner, N. and R. Busch
1962 Field Fragmentation in a Tertiary Area. Fourth Regional Irrigation Seminar. Ankara.

Urquhart, D.
1833 Turkey and Its Resources. London.

Volney, C. F.
1787 Voyage en Egypte et en Syrie pendant les annees 1783, 1784 et 1785. Paris.

Von Oppenheim, M. F.
1939 Die Beduinen Vol. I. Leipsig.

Ward, N.
1952 Antakya. Brasil. (Arabic)

Warriner, D.
    1948   Land and Poverty in the Middle East. London.
    1957   Land Reforms and Development in the Middle East. London.
Weulersse, J.
    1934   Antioche, essai de geographie urbain. Bull. d'Et. Orient. L'Institut Français de Damas.
    1940   Le Pays des Alaouites. Tours.
    1946   Paysans de Syrie et du Proche Orient. Paris.
Whitten, N.
    1969   Strategies of Adaptive Mobility in the Colombian-Ecuadorian Litteral. American Anthropologist Vol. 71:228-42.
Williams, H. H. and J. R. Williams
    1965   The Extended Family as a Vehicle of Culture Change. Human Organization, 24:59-64.
Wittek, P.
    1952   Le role des tribes Turques dans l'empire Ottoman. Melanges Georges Smets. Pp. 554-70. Brussels.
Wolf, E.
    1956   Aspects of Group Relations in a Complex Society: Mexico. American Anthropologist 58:1065-78.
    1957   Closed Corporate Peasant Communities in Mesoamerica and Central Java. Southwestern Journal of Anthropology XIII, No. 1:7-12.
    1966   Peasants. New Jersey.
    1969   Peasants Wars of the Twentieth Century. Harper and Row. New York.
Zetlzer, M.
    1962   Aspects of Near Eastern Society. New York.
Zenner, W.
    1966   Alternative Political Ideals in the Fertile Crescent. Paper presented at Central States Anthropological Society. St. Louis.

Bay of Iskenderun and Amanus Mountain Range.

View of a Village.

Typical Home of Al Shiukh.

House of a Worker or Sharecropper.

PLATE V

a. Guest Room (Oda), Villagers, Teachers and Coffee Utensils.

b. Respected Shaykh in Oda.

Women at the Well.

PLATE VII

Storage Bins and Outside Kitchen for Wife of Al Shiukh.

PLATE VIII

a. Outside Kitchen for Wife of Shepherd.

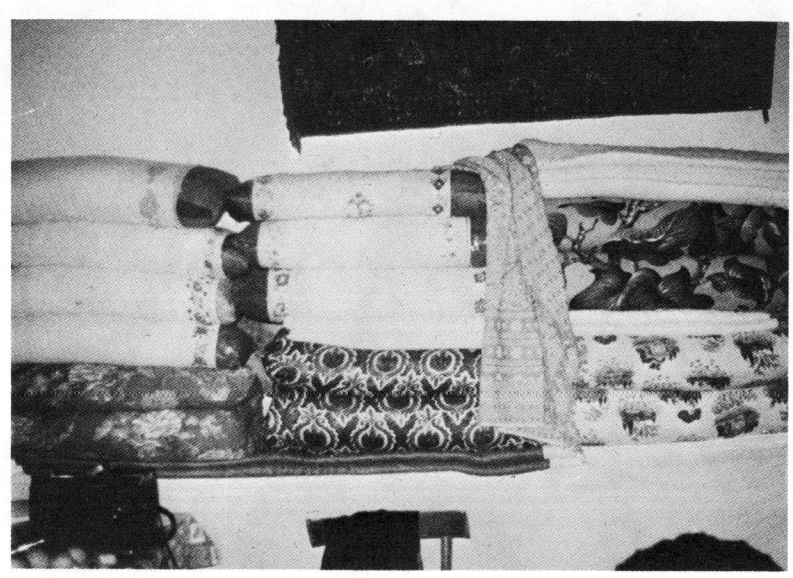

b. Stacked bedding.

PLATE IX

Seeding in the Traditional Method.

a. Rented Tractors.

b. Traditional Scratch Plow and Saluqi Dog.

PLATE XI

a. Cotton Laden on Trucks in the Region.

b. The Town Market.

Measuring Land Divisions with Ropes.

Grinding Grain in the Traditional Method.

Bee Hives.

Village School.

Boys going to the City to Trade School and the Lise.

Dancing the Debke at a Wedding.